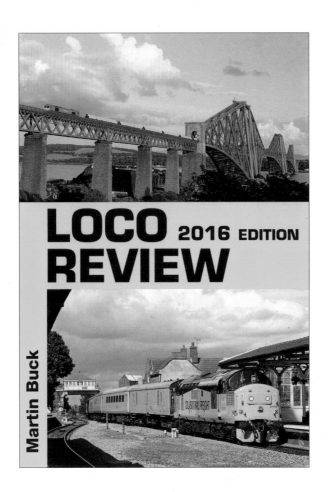

LOCO 2016 EDITION
REVIEW

Martin Buck

FREIGHTMASTER

PUBLISHING

Contents

ISBN : 978-0-9933129-0-8

Published, November 2015 :

Freightmaster Publishing
158 Overbrook
SWINDON
SN3 6AY

www.freightmasterpublishing.co.uk

Printed By :

Stephens & George
Goat Mill Road
Dowlais
MERTHYR TYDFIL
CF48 3TD

www.stephensandgeorge.co.uk

Note : All dates in the text are 2015, unless otherwise stated.

Setting the Scene

Welcome to *Loco Review 2016* ....

.... and warm congratulations go to the Forth Rail Bridge in being accorded *'World Heritage'* status; this fabulous feat of Victorian engineering takes pride of place on the front cover.

As in previous editions, there's a wide-ranging selection of topics, illustrated by quality images, with contributions by some of the best railway photographers around. My thanks go to all contributors, your assistance is very much appreciated.

With only a limited number of pages with which to play, it's never easy deciding on content. For example, 50 years have elapsed since the first Class 86 ACL loco rolled off the Vulcan Foundry production line at Newton-Le-Willows in 1965 and 25 years since the last member of the Class 90 fleet (No.90050) entered service, quite appropriately in 1990.

So, I've opted for the Class 90 and 30 pages devoted to passenger and freight duties with which the Class has been associated.

These versatile locos are often overshadowed by their Class 86 and 87 counterparts and have, perhaps, been unfairly dubbed 'Skodas' by enthusiasts (you can decide for yourself what this means!). It's time they had a spell in the spotlight.

A leading industrialist once said "the only constant in life is change" and this is certainly true of the railways. Who would have thought 'heritage' traction would still have an important role to play today.

DRS Class 37s have been introduced on timetabled passenger services on the Cumbrian Coast and in East Anglia, plus Colas are resurrecting more Class 60s. The 'new kids on the block' UKRL (United Kingdom Rail Leasing) have now entered the railfreight sector, initially hiring out refurbished Class 56s - how many enthusiasts still think "nothing ever changes".

The 'new' Class 68s have now bedded in on Chiltern passenger services and the 'Fife Circle' commuter trains and, having sampled these fine locos first hand, I can see why DRS have decided to order some more.

The design is aesthetically pleasing on the eye, they are powerful and sound good too - no doubt other operators will soon realise their capabilities.

Please forgive me, but I have included a new section - *'On this Day'* - to celebrate some notable events that have taken place in 2015. Not all of them have a railway theme, but I feel they are worth mentioning.

Following on from the last issue, I am pleased to conclude with a *'Gallery'* section, to show off some more stunning images, ones which would otherwise slip through the net as they do not fit into the topics being covered. They show what excellent results can be achieved with a little thought and imagination - I hope you agree and make sure you look out for a couple of surprise images along the way!

Martin Buck

A 'Barbie' liveried, and one of the 'football team', GBRf Class 66/7 No.**66725** '**Sunderland**' (above) has just passed Embsay Junction on 20th November 2014 with 6M83, the 11:10 Rylstone - Wellingborough loaded limestone. The consist is a rake of former Freightliner branded 'MJA' box wagons.

No.66725 became the first GBRf Class 66/7 loco to be named after a football team; *'Sunderland'*, on 10th August 2007 by the then chairman of Sunderland football club, Mr Niall Quinn, at a ceremony held at the Port of Tyne.   **Neil Harvey**

Background

Prior to securing the Bardon traffic (described later), GBRf venture onto new metals by hauling limestone trains along the Grassington Branch, from Swinden quarry at Rylstone to terminals at Wellingborough and Small Heath. The first train runs on 5th November 2014.

6M19,	**Rylstone - Small Heath**	GBRf Class 66/7	**Bogie Box Wagons**
6M19,	**Rylstone - Wellingborough**	GBRf Class 66/7	**Bogie Box Wagons**

This new flow (originally coded 6M83) provides an opportunity to take a close look at this traffic, along with traction associated with this branch line, both past and present.

History

Known locally as 'The Yorkshire Dales Railway', a branch line links the market town of Skipton with the villages of Rylstone, Threshfield and Grassington, albeit now 'freight only'. There were two stations on the line - Grassington & Threshfield and Rylstone - and the line was authorised by Act of Parliament in August 1897, opening 29th July 1902, operated by the Midland Railway.

Regular passenger services ceased on 22nd September 1930, but the line remained open for freight traffic, albeit only as far as Swinden Quarry, which now regularly despatches trainloads of limestone to terminals in Leeds and Hull.

The station at Grassington was built as a through station, although being a terminus, there were plans to extend the line northwards to Hawes, where it would meet the Wensleydale Railway. This never materialised.

Swinden Quarry Departures - Weekdays

Time	Code	Train	Traction	Notes	
03:53	6D71	Rylstone - Hull Dairycoates	DBS 66		
11:10	6M19	Rylstone - Wellingborough	GBRf 66	MFX	
11:10	6M19	Rylstone - Small Heath	GBRf 66	ThO	
11:10	6M19	Rylstone - Stourton Junction	GBRf 66	ThO	(as required)
18:13	6D73	Rylstone - Leeds Hunslet	DBS 66		
21:10	6N59	Rylstone - Redcar BSC Terminal	DBS 66		

Freight Services

A 'snapshot' of departures from Rylstone is given above and access to and from the branch line can only be effected after reversal at Skipton.

Route	Location	Milepost Mileage
	RYLSTONE	**7.09**
	Embsay Junction	0.00 / 220.64*
	Haw Bank Tunnel	220.77 - 221.07
	Keighley Road Viaduct	224.24 - 224.27
	Skipton Middle Junction	221.33
	Down Shipley Slow Line	-
	Skipton Middle Junction	221.33
	Skipton	**221.21**

* Mileage from London St. Pancras via Ilkley.

(Above) : An immaculate Class 66, No.66768 is seen at Stourton, Leeds, on 25th February with 6M19, the 11:10 Rylstone Tilcon - Wellingborough Up TC limestone.

No.66768 was one of seven new 'Bluebirds' (Nos.66766 - 66772) shipped across the Atlantic Ocean to Newport Docks in December 2014. Sister loco No.66706 'Nene Valley' towed the new locos in convoy (0X66) to Doncaster Roberts Road on 9th December 2014.   **Pauline McKenna**

(Top Left) : On a glorious, frosty, 3rd February, No.66705 *'Golden Jubilee'* climbs past Rylstone village with 6M19 loaded limestone. This loco was named to commemorate the 50th anniversary of Her Majesty the Queen's accession to the throne and is known as 'The Flag' for obvious reasons.   **Neil Harvey**

(Bottom Left) : The GBRf Rylstone limestone traffic commences on 5th November 2014 and Class 66/7 No.66755 has charge of the first service (6M83) to Small Heath. It is passing the site of Goose Hill Junction, Normanton, where the ex-Midland main line branches off to run direct to Sheffield.

From here 6M19 is routed:

Turners Lane Jct. - Calder Bridge Jct. - Hare Park Jct. - South Elmsall - Doncaster - Hexthorpe Jct. - Mexborough - Masborough Jct. - Beighton Jct. - Chesterfield - Ambergate - Derby - Long Eaton - Trent South Jct. - East Midlands Parkway - Loughborough - Leicester - Kettering - Wellingborough. **Derek Holmes**

Rylstone 'Heritage' Traction

During the late 1990s and early 'noughties', occasional flows of limestone ran from Rylstone to Dewsbury, using EWS 'Monster' bogie box wagons, coded 'MBA'. On 1st May 2001, Transrail Class 56 No 56025 (above) is seen near Scale House with 6G97, the 09:20 Rylstone - Dewsbury; the newly born lambs don't seem worried by the train's passing. A total of 200 'MBAs' were built in 1999 by Thrall, York.

Class 60s were once a regular sight on the branch before the arrival of DBS 'sheds'. On 16th February 1996, No 60067 'James Clark Maxwell' (above) looks impressive on the embankment near Ellergill House on the Rylstone branch with 6D72, the 11:32 Hull Dairycoates - Rylstone. A batch of 33, 2-Axle, aggregate hoppers were built for Tilcon by BREL, Shildon, during 1973, specifically for this traffic.

In 1994, new 'JGA' bogie covered hoppers were built by Powell Duffryn, SA, France, to replace the incumbent hoppers on the limestone flows to Hull and Leeds, numbered NACO 19170 - NACO 19199. A rake of these 'COVHOPS' is the consist for celebrity Class 60 No 60081 'Isambard Kingdom Brunel' (above), which is passing Scale House on 7th March 1995 with 6D72, the 11:18 Hull Dairycoates - Rylstone.

Truly, a majestic sight. Prior to the introduction of Class 60s - Class 37s and 31s were regular performers on the 'Tilcon' traffic. On 7th March 1992, Class 37/5s, No.37686 + No.37688 'Great Rocks' (below), having run round their train at Skipton, prepare to head up to Rylstone with 6D75 empties from Leeds. Alas, No.37686 was cut up at CF Booth, Rotherham, in 2006. Happily, No.37688 is still going strong for DRS and has been in use on the Cumbrian Coast Northern Rail loco hauled services. **Neil Harvey (4)**

Up close and personal: an impressive shot of GBRf Class 66/7 No.66755 (above) approaching the foot crossing just south of Adwick-le-Street station on 1st April with 6M19, the 11:10 Rylstone - Wellingborough loaded stone. Note the two new blue GBRf 'MJA' bogie hoppers behind the loco.
Alan Padley

Meanwhile, Class 31/1s No.**31247** + No.**31162** (below) run into Skipton station with a Saturday afternoon 'Tilcon' train from Hull. Note the steam-age railway paraphernalia very much in evidence as late as 16th May 1987. Of course, the approach to Skipton station doesn't look like this now, the semaphores have long gone, so too the water pump. It's now colour light signalling and a canopy of overhead electrification wires!
Neil Harvey

Bardon goes over to GBRf

Background

From January, GBRf extend their share of the aggregate market by taking over flows of stone emanating from the Bardon / Croft quarries in the East Midlands on behalf of Aggregate Industries. The trains were previously operated by Freightliner Heavy Haul.

Service	*1st Train*
- Bardon Hill / Croft to Neasden	Tuesday, 6th January
- Bardon Hill to Tinsley	Tuesday, 6th January
- Bardon Hill to Colnbrook	Tuesday, 6th January
- Bardon Hill to Angerstein	Wednesday, 7th January
Plus;	
- Grain to Neasden	Wednesday, 7th January
- Neath - Angerstein	Wednesday, 7th January
- Shrewsbury Coton Hill to Theale	Thursday, 8th January
- Avonmouth to Colnbrook	Friday, 9th January

The actual trainplan is complex involving five sets of wagons, as set out on pages 14 and 15.

Freight traffic routed on the Midland main Line via Sheffield Midland is not a common occurrence, so this image is a welcome inclusion .... on 11th March, GBRf Class 66/7 No.66730 'Whitemoor' (above) departs from Heeley 'Up Passenger Loop', two miles south of Sheffield Midland station with 6M01, the 10:51 Tinsley Yard - Bardon Hill empty stone train.   **Ian Ball**

No.66758 (above) passes through East Midlands Parkway on 11th February with 6M01, 10:51 Tinsley - Bardon Hill. East Midlands Parkway station is situated just three minutes from the M1 Motorway (Jct. 24) close to Ratcliffe-on-Soar power station.   **Alan Hazelden**

A deserted platform greets No.66758 (below), as it stops very briefly on platform 7 for a crew change on 9th February with 6Z33, the 21:10 Shrewsbury Coton Hill - Cardiff Pengam loaded stone. This train will go forward from Cardiff the next day to Theale, under a 6Z34 reporting code.   **Mike Hemming**

GBRf / Bardon Diagrams

		Loaded	Empty
Monday	:	6O59, Bardon Hill - Angerstein	6V43, to Cardiff Pengam
Tuesday	:		6C39, Pengam - Avonmouth
		6A40, Avonmouth - Pengam	
Wednesday	:	6A28, Pengam - Colnbrook	6B11 return
Thursday	:		6C38, Pengam - Avonmouth
		6A39, Avonmouth - Pengam	
Friday	:	6A28, Pengam - Colnbrook	6B11 return

		Loaded	Empty
Monday	:		6B42, Pengam - Neath
		6B75, Neath - Pengam	
Tuesday	:	6O55, Pengam - Angerstein	6M82, to Bardon Hill
Wednesday	:	6O59, Bardon Hill - Angerstein	6M79, return
Thursday	:	6V48, Bardon Hill - Colnbrook	6M54, return
Friday	:	6O59, Bardon Hill - Angerstein	6M79, return

		Loaded	Empty
Tuesday	:	6E48, Bardon Hill - Tinsley	6M01, return
Wednesday	:	6E48, Bardon Hill - Tinsley	6Z32, to Coton Hill
		6Z33, Coton Hill - Pengam	
Thursday	:	6Z34, Pengam - Theale	6Z54, to Bardon Hill
Friday	:	6E48, Bardon Hill - Tinsley	6M01 return

		Loaded	Empty
Monday	:	6M28, Bardon Hill - Neasden	6M47, to Croft
Wednesday	:	6M25, Croft - Neasden	6M47, to Croft
Thursday	:	6L18, Croft - Harlow Mill	6M14, to Bardon Hill

		Loaded	Empty
Monday	:	6Z90, Tonbridge - Grain	
Tuesday	:	6M90, Grain - Neasden	6O69, return
Wednesday	:	6V89, Grain - Brentford	6M70, to Neasden
			6O69, Neasden - Grain
Thursday	:	6E48, Grain - Brentford,	6M70, to Neasden
			6O69, Neasden - Grain
Friday	:	6E48, Grain - Neasden	6O69, to Tonbridge

Wagon Sets

The new GBRf / Bardon diagrams require five sets of bogie hopper wagons:

Set 1
JGA :

BHQ 17149	BHQ 17143	BHQ 17132	BHQ 17144	BHQ 17148	BHQ 17147	BHQ 17125
BHQ 17138	BHQ 17120	BHQ 17101	BHQ 17135	BHQ 17122	BHQ 17151	BHQ 17107
BHQ 17145	BHQ 17134	BHQ 17141	BHQ 17124			70.6905.058-7* (***JRA**)

Set 2
JGA :

BHQ 17105	BHQ 17113	BHQ 17109	BHQ 17102	BHQ 17142	BHQ 17108	BHQ 17117
BHQ 17116	BHQ 17115	BHQ 17112	BHQ 17118	BHQ 17127	BHQ 17110	BHQ 17104
BHQ 17121	BHQ 17119	BHQ 17123	BHQ 17114	BHQ 17129	BHQ 17106	

Set 3
JGA :

AI 27106	AI 27117	AI 27108	AI 27122	AI 27121	AI 27101	AI 27110
AI 27119	AI 27113	AI 27118	AI 27109	AI 27103	AI 27111	AI 27114
AI 27120	AI 27112	AI 27105	AI 27102			

Set 4
JRA :

70.6905.062-9	70.6905.073-6	70.6905.050-4	70.6905.071-0	70.6905.065-2	70.6905.068-6
70.6905.067-8	70.6905.059-5	70.6905.051-2	70.6905.072-8	70.6905.057-9	70.6905.056-1
70.6905.070-2	70.6905.069-4	70.6905.055-3	70.6905.066-0	70.6905.063-7	
BHQ 17140*	BHQ 17130*	AI 27104*			(***JGAs**)

Set 5
JGA :

ERG 17305	ERG 17315	ERG 17302	ERG 17321	ERG 17324	ERG 17316	ERG 17317
ERG 17304	ERG 17318	ERG 17312	ERG 17314	ERG 17306	ERG 17308	ERG 17319
ERG 17303	ERG 17320	ERG 17310	ERG 17311	ERG 17313		

On 23rd January, No.66736 'Wolverhampton Wanderers' (above) weaves through the alterations being made between Plumstead and Abbey Wood, whilst working 6M79, the 11:56 Angerstein Wharf - Bardon Hill, formed mainly of 'JRAs', recently repainted in blue livery. **Ian Cuthbertson**

No.66713 (top left) heads 6V43, the 11:56 Angerstein - Cardiff Pengam along the embankment at South Marston, Swindon, on 10th April. Unrestricted views, such as this one, will soon become consigned to history with the spread of electrification on the GWML. **Martin Buck**

At the time, the latest member of the Class 66/7 fleet, No.**66769** (left), heads away from Bexley on 27th February with 6O69, the 09:45 Neasden - Tonbridge Yard stone empties.

The consist is a rake of former Freightliner Heavy Haul 'Jolly Green Giants', otherwise known as 'JGA' bogie aggregate hoppers, numbered:

FLHH 17302 - 17324

These wagons were biult in 1987 by W H Davis, Shirebrook.

Stuart Chapman

The loco diagrams for these new flows are complex and a total of six GBRf Class 66/7s are needed to work the respective flows. Here are the details for train 6Z32, which is shown above:

(1) 6E48, 01:28 Bardon Hill - Tinsley Yard   6M01, 10:51 Tinsley Yard - Bardon Hill

(2) 6E48, 01:28 Bardon Hill - Tinsley Yard   6Z32, 10:51 Tinsley Yard - Shrewsbury Coton Hill

                                                6Z33, 21:12 Coton Hill - Pengam

(3) 6Z34, 01:50 Pengam - Theale Lafarge   6Z54, 11:45 Theale Lafarge - Bardon Hill

(4) 6O59, 00:19 Bardon Hill - Angerstein   6V43, 11:56 Angerstein Wharf - Pengam

On 8th January, GBRf Class 66/7 No.'**66701** '**Whitemoor**' (above), hauls the first 6Z32, 10:51 Tinsley - Shrewsbury Coton Hill, which is seen heading west past Duncote Mill, Walcot, with empty hoppers. The train will be loaded to go forward as 6Z33, 21:10 Coton Hill - Cardiff Pengam the next day.   **Mike Hemming**

'BICESTER CHORD'

Background : In August 2008, Chiltern Railways announced 'Project Evergreen 3' to create a new passenger service between Oxford and London Marylebone via High Wycombe.

Part of this project includes opening a short *'missing-link'* from Bicester Town station to the Chiltern Main Line, providing Oxford with a direct rail-link to High Wycombe for the first time since BR closed the Princes Risborough - Oxford section of the Wycombe Railway in 1964.

The work involves:
 - constructing a new Chord, connecting OXD to NAJ-3 lines at Bicester.
 - Bicester Town – Woodstock Road Junction line completely rebuilt.
 - double track.
 - new signalling controlled from London Marylebone.
 - rebuild Islip and Bicester Town station.
 - new Parkway station at Water Orton, called Oxford Parkway.
 - improved freight facilities at Banbury Road Sidings and MOD Bicester.

Freight Services : While this work is carried out, freight services using the single section of line from Oxford North Junction via Islip to Bicester have to be diverted. In practice, this affects just two Ministry of Defence 'trips':

6A49, 07:32	Didcot Yard - Bicester	EWS 66 / 67	MoD stores
6A48, 12:59	Bicester - Didcot Yard	EWS 66 / 67	MoD stores

Details of the diversionary route are :

6A49 diversion

Location	Pass		Location	Pass
DIDCOT T.C.	**07:32**		South Ruislip	09:35
Didcot East Jct.	07:37	RL	West Ruislip	09:38
Goring & Streatley	07:49		Gerrards Cross	09:45
Reading	**08:02**	URL	**High Wycombe**	**09:58**
Twyford	08:08		Saunderton	10:05
Maidenhead	08:19	RL	Princes Risborough	10:12
Slough	08:33	RL	Little Kimble	10:18
Iver	08:41	GL	Aylesbury	10:30
West Drayton	08:48 - 09:02 RL		Aylesbury North Loop	10:34 - 10:44
Heathrow Airport Jct.	09:06	RL	Aylesbury Vale Parkway	10:49
Southall	09:10	RL	Calvert	11:06
Hanwell	09:15		Claydon L.N.E. Jct.	11:24 - 11:44
Drayton Green	09:17		Bicester London Rd L.C.	12:08 - 12:13
Greenford South Jct.	09:22		**BICESTER C.O.D.**	**12:15**
Greenford West Jct.	09:24			

Abbreviations

GL = Goods Loop	RL = Relief Line	URL = Up Relief Line

The new 'chord' is completed in late September and driver training runs start in October.

6A49

Arriva blue Class 67 No.67003 (above) passes Cholsey on 28 April 2015 with the diverted 6A49, 07:32 Didcot - Bicester MoD stores and a good load on this occasion, as it would not be at all uncommon for the train to consist of just the two 'VGA' vans! This train has to take a very long way round, going via Greenford and Calvert. Note the stanchions for GWML electrification. **Martin Loader**

On 12th March, another Class 67 is atop 6A49, seen approaching the foot-crossing at Park Mill Farm having just come on to the branch to Aylesbury at Princes Risborough. This MoD 'trip' produces a good variety of motive power and today it's DBS No.67018 'Keith Heller' (below) doing the honours. **Geoff Plumb**

The 'Bicester Chord'

On 6th October, a Network Rail test train (1Q05), top and tailed by DRS Class 37/4s No.37605 and No.37604 (above), stands on the new chord between Bicester Gavray Junction and Bicester South Junction, awaiting a path south to return to Old Oak Common. Class 68 No.68013 is passing northbound with DVT No.82303 on the rear of 1R15, the 08:45 London Marylebone - Birmingham Moor Street, whilst an unidentified Class 165 is southbound with 1H30, the 09:06 from Banbury to Marylebone.

This is, perhaps, the first "proper" revenue earning train over the new chord - 6A48, the 12:20 Bicester C.O.D. - Didcot Yard, which is still routed 'the long way round' as the more direct route via Islip and Oxford has not been cleared for traffic.. On 28th September, DBS Class 66/0 No.66113 (below) has just passed over Bicester Gavray Junction and is on the new chord with a long rake of 'VGA' vans and container flats in tow. The tracks over to the right lead towards Claydon and Bletchley and, as you can see, groundwork beside the chord near the new footbridge is still ongoing. **Geoff Plumb (2)**

OXFORD - BICESTER : Colas Class 70 No.70804 (above) is on the Oxford end of a ballast train while, on the other side of the bridge carrying the Chiltern Main Line, is No.70809 on the Bletchley end of a rake of ballast wagons for the new chord. The train is 6C32, the 22:58 Hinksey Yard - Claydon L&NE Junction, running via Banbury, Princes Risborough and Aylesbury.

Colas Rail Class 70 No.70809 (below) stands in the new station undergoing construction at Islip on 6th May with a trainload of sleepers being unloaded. This train has worked in from Claydon L&NE Junction, as the first of the new tracks was complete by this time and the second track was in the process of being laid. The new platforms still have to be completed. This view is looking towards Bicester.   **Geoff Plumb (2)**

Islip : The new trackbed, freshly covered with a layer of brilliant white ballast, at Islip on 21st April, is yet more preparatory work as part of Chiltern's new route to London, and for the East West Rail project. This is the cutting between the two road bridges, a location that was formerly very overgrown, hardly recognisable from the same view in 2012 .....

Flashback Class 56 No.**56301** (below) passes through a frosty landscape at Islip on 13th December 2012 with 6Z91, the 10:53 Calvert - Didcot power station flyash empties. Despite the freezing cold and gloomy conditions, the photographer wasn't going to miss the chance of getting a picture of the 'Grid' in this typical winter setting! Islip station is just beyond the bridge in the background.   **Martin Loader (2)**

HARBURY

Background

Major landslips seem to be coming in threes during the winter months; Hatfield Colliery (February 2013), Dawlish (February 2014) and now Harbury in January 2015.

Network Rail take the decision to close the route between Leamington Spa and Banbury, outside the north portal of Harbury Tunnel, to determine the scale of the landslip; an initial assessment reported around 350,000 tonnes of material on the embankment near the tunnel would need to be removed.

The area outside Harbury Tunnel is a known problem area, where there are elevated levels of ground water. In fact, when the landslide happened, Network Rail were carrying out stabilisation work after a smaller landslip on the site in February 2014 (see opposite).

Train Services

Passenger : Chiltern Railway and Aviva Cross Country routes have been affected and a revised service has been put in place between Banbury and Marylebone, Birmingham and Leamington Spa, and Stratford-upon-Avon and Leamington Spa.

Freight : Most freight services have been diverted via the WCML, some cancelled altogether, plus a few (see table) diverted 'off the beaten track', notably via the Cotswold Line (Oxford - Worcester, via Moreton in Marsh) and the Golden Valley (Standish Jct. - Swindon, via Kemble).

Harbury Diversions - Weekdays

Evesham

Time	Code	Train	Traction	Notes
13:22	6M50	07:55 Westbury - Bescot	Colas 70	Departmental
21:59	6V46	19:00 Bescot - Westbury	Colas 70	Departmental

Kemble

Time	Code	Train	Traction	Notes
03:53	6V85	02:00 Milford West Sidings - Appleford	DBS 66	Containerised Flyash
06:24	6V22	02:00 Liverpool Euro. Metal - Swindon	DBS 66	Empty Scrap
18:16	6M28	17:16 Hinksey - Bescot	FHH 66	Departmental
20:17	6E03	16:48 Appleford - Milford West Sidings	DBS 66	Empty Flyash

History

The deep, curving cutting, about 1.5 miles long has the 73 yard Harbury Tunnel at its heart, which supports the B4452 road north of Harbury. The line was built for the Birmingham and Oxford Junction Railway (Broad Gauge) between 1847 and 1852, reportedly by Isambard Kingdom Brunel.

It was originally intended for a longer tunnel to be built, but unstable ground resulted in a cutting 110 feet deep being constructed instead; the deepest man-made cutting in the world at the time. The cutting itself was widened around 1884 because of soil slippage – a problem that has not been entirely solved to this day.

The line became part of the Great Western Railway and was the main route taken by London Paddington to Wolverhampton and Birkenhead passenger expresses. The last services to both Wolverhampton Low Level and Birkenhead ran in 1968 and 1967, respectively.

Re-opening

The main line re-opens on Saturday, 15th March.

Courtesy Network Rail

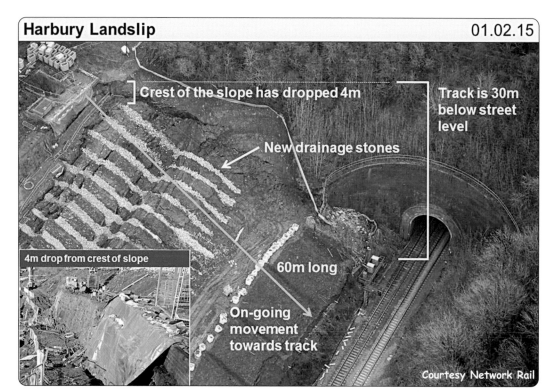

Crest of the slope has dropped 4m

Track is 30m below street level

New drainage stones

4m drop from crest of slope

60m long

On-going movement towards track

Courtesy Network Rail

NOTABLE DIVERTS

6M25 .... 'Rainbow Warrior' GBRf Class 66/7 No.66720 (below) passes Ram Hill, three miles east of Bristol Parkway station, on 2nd March with the diverted 6M25, 09:16 Westbury TC - Cliffe Hill Stud Farm empty 'Gondola' ballast wagons. This train will leave the GWML at Westerleigh Junction and head northwards via Cheltenham, Longbridge, Landor Street Jct., Water Orton, Nuneaton and Knighton Jct. in order to reach its destination. The loaded service (6V14) uses the same route. **Chris Perkins**

6V85 .... identifies the 02:00 Milford West Sidings - Appleford, which conveys flyash from Drax power station for depositing in a landfill site at Appleford, adjacent to the Didcot - Oxford main line.

Flyash workings are not usually seen at Swindon and as 6V85 is booked to run overnight, photo opportunities are rare, save for when there is late running, as on a dull 11th March. DBS Class 66/0 No.66101 is first seen coming off the 'Gloucester Line' (above) and then accelarating towards Highworth Junction (below), having made a pathing stop in the station. Note the GWML electrification MPVs. **Martin Buck (2)**

6042 : On the embankment alongside the A420 road at South Marston, DBS No.66074 (above) heads towards Swindon on 10th April with 6042, the diverted 11:42 Halewood - Southampton Eastern Docks empty 'IPA' (4384s) car carriers. Fortunately, no high-sided lorries decided to pass at the same time! **Martin Buck**

4070 : The diverted Wentloog freightliner is seen on 3rd April passing through the Wylye Valley at Little Langford with Class 70 No.70019 (below) at the helm. Note the magnificent Little Langford farmhouse (c.1858), which has a Victorian Gothic entrance tower, lancet windows and crenellations. **Mark Pike**

6M50

Colas 70s
on the
COTSWOLD LINE

The closure of the route through Harbury Cutting results in the Colas operated 6M50, 07:55 Westbury - Bescot being diverted after Oxford, via the Cotswold Line to Worcester and up the 'Lickey' to reach its destination.

The train is booked Class 70 traction and can start from either Westbury or Hinksey Yard (Oxford).

With no scheduled freight services along the Oxford - Worcester line, save for Long Marston wagon moves and weekend engineering 'trips', the chance to photograph a 'real freight' on this line is a bonus.

The Cotswold Line runs for some 41 miles between the following junctions:

Wolvercote Jct. Milepost 66m. 32chs.

Norton Jct.   Milepost 117m. 26chs.

The Mileposts show the mileage from London Paddington (via Didcot station, Oxford, Worcester Shrub Hill, Worcester Foregate Street, Great Malvern and Ledbury) to Shelwick Jct. (Milepost 148m. 11chs.), where this line meets the Newport - Shrewsbury main line.

The Cotswold line was also affectionately known as the "Old Worse and Worse" - the Oxford, Worcester and Wolverhampton line!

(inset) :

Moreton-in-Marsh

Passing some lower quadrant GWR semaphore signals, a convoy consisting No.70806 leading, Nos.70808 & 70805, plus No.59201 approaches the railway station with 6Z50, the 12:46 Hinksey Yard - Bescot departmental.

Geoff Plumb

Diverted 6M50, 07:55 Westbury - Bescot

Location	Pass	Arr.	Dep.
WESTBURY DOWN TC		07:55	
WESTBURY	07:59		
Bradford Jct.	08:09		
Thingley Jct.	08:24		
CHIPPENHAM	08:29		
SWINDON	08:52		
Highworth Jct. UGL		08:56	09:16
Wantage Road		09:38	09:58
Steventon	10:05		
Foxhall Jct.		10:11	10:36
Didcot North Jct.	10:41		
Hinksey Sidings		10:55	12:46
OXFORD	12:52		
Wolvercote Jct.	12:57		
Charlbury		13:06	
Ascott-under-Wychwood	13:11		
MORETON-IN-MARSH	13:25		
Honeybourne	13:34		
EVESHAM	13:41		
Norton Jct.	13:53		
WORCESTER SHRUB HILL	14:00		
DROITWICH SPA		14:12	13:20
Stoke Works Jct..	14:26		
Bromsgrove Up Goods Loop		14:29	14:45
Bromsgrove	14:47		
Barnt Green	14:58		
Longbridge	15:15		
Kings Norton	15:21		
Lifford East Jct.	15:23		
Landor Street Jct.		15:33	15;36
Castle Bromwich Jct.	15:49		
Park Lane Jct.		15:52	16:03
Ryecroft Jct.	16:23		
WALSALL	16:25		
Pleck Jct.	16:28		
Bescot Jct.	16:30		
BESCOT ENGINEER SDGS.			16:35

LYNEHAM : On 9th February, No.70803 (above) passes Lyneham with 6M50, the 07:55 Westbury - Bescot, which had been held at Didcot for some considerable time and was 92 minutes late approaching Oxford. However, by missing out its normal layover in Hinksey Yard, it converted the late running into being 47 minutes early by the time it passed through Oxford station. Note the mole activity!

ASCOTT-UNDER-WYCHWOOD : No.70807 (below) passes through Ascott-under-Wychwood station on 18th February with 6M50 from Westbury. Amongst all the modern signage and station furniture, there is a reminder of GWR days, with provision of GWR style station seats. **Martin Loader (2)**

SHIPTON : A convoy of Nos.70806, 70808, 70805 and 59201 (above) is seen on 6th February, passing through Shipton station with 6Z50 ex-Hinksey. On this occasion, a dull day enables a picture to be taken from the north side of the line, allowing the station nameboard to be included in the image. **Martin Loader**

WORCESTER : On 11th February, the 12th century Worcester Cathedral is silhouetted against a grey sky, as No.70805 (below) approaches Worcester Tunnel Junction at the head of 6Z50 from Westbury. The actual tunnel is 154 yards north of here, entitled Rainbow Hill, and is 212 yards in length. **Chris Davies**

4055

Temporarily re-routed to the Sleaford line as a result of the Harbury landslip, 4055, 12:12 Leeds FLT - Southampton freightliner makes its way slowly over High Street level crossing on the approach to Lincoln central station in the hands of Class 66/5 No.66589 (above), on Friday, 13th March. This proves to be the final day of its diversionary route.

From a historical perspective, Network Rail instituted a major resignalling scheme for Lincoln Central during the years 2007 – 2008 which resulted in:

- the replacement of the semaphore signals with colour light signals.
- four existing signal boxes closed: High Street, East Holmes, West Holmes and Pelham Street Junction.
- a new state of the art signalling centre opened near West Holmes box.
- track relaying, new points and crossovers to allow bi-directional running.

David Hayes

6X01

During the diversions, many freights are being sent via London 'under the wires' by way of either the ECML or the WCML. On 23rd February, DBS Class 60 No.60062 'Stainless Pioneer' (above) has been directed via the ECML after leaving Doncaster and is seen approaching Sandy, ambling along the 'Up Slow' line, with the diverted 6X01, 10:17 Scunthorpe Trent T.C - Eastleigh East Yard loaded rails.

6M48

DBS Class 66/0 No.66017 (below) passes Soulbury Road on the WCML (7th March) with a rake of covered car carriers, which form 6M48, the 09:58 Southampton Eastern Docks - Halewood. Note the loco has DB stickers with the EWS logo removed from the body side.   **Nigel Gibbs (2)**

4070 : The driver piles on the power, as Class 70 No.70004 (above) departs Salisbury on 10th April with the diverted 4070 09:58 Cardiff Wentloog - Southampton Maritime freightliner. The train has reached this point via Patchway - Lawrence Hill - North Somerset Jct. - Bath - Westbury - Warminster.

4015 : After leaving Salisbury station, the diverted services head for Romsey via Fisherton Tunnel - Salisbury Tunnel Junction - Laverstock South Junction On 3rd April, Freightliner's Class 66/5 No.66501 (below) exits the tunnel at Salisbury Tunnel Junction with 4015, the diverted 07:43 Hams Hall Parsec - Southampton 'liner. Fisherton Tunnel is 443 yards long. **Mark Pike (2)**

READING 'BLOCKADE'

Background

January heralds several months of weekend 'blockades' in the Reading area for major remodelling work.

This results in the closure of Reading West Curve between Reading West Junction and Oxford Road Junction.

On a Saturday and a full two weeks at Easter, freight services using this route are diverted:

Freightliners / DBS Intermodal
via WCML, London, Maidenhead.

Departmental services and Cars
via Swindon, Westbury, Salisbury.

Theale 'Murco' tanks / 6V62 steel
via the 'Berks. & Hants.'

Weekday Diversions ~ Salisbury

Code	Train			PASS
6M38	23:23	Southampton E. D.	Halewood	01:56
4V51	03:12	Southampton	Cardiff Wentloog	01:55
4M19	00:58	Southampton	Daventry	02:04
4V30	23:00	Tilbury	Bristol FLT	03:32
4E01	02:15	Southampton	Leeds	03:49
4V36	23:34	Felixstowe North	Bristol FLT	05:21
4011	00:23	Crewe Basford Hall	Southampton	06:31
4012	02:40	Lawley Street	Southampton	07:24
6O15	17:27	Mossend yard	Eastleigh Yard	07:57
4O22	01:47	Trafford Park	Southampton	08:10
4012	02:40	Lawley Street	Southampton	09:09
6M66	09:32	Southampton W D	Garston	10:32
6M48	10:34	Southampton E D	Halewood	11:52
6O26	10:19	Hinksey Yard	Eastleigh Yard	12:11
4015	07:43	Hams Hall	Southampton	12:20
4070	09:58	Cardiff Wentloog	Southampton	13:40
4054	06:12	Leeds	Southampton	14:59
4049	09:22	Crewe Basford Hall	Southampton	15:40
4027	05:36	Garston	Southampton	17:03
6X01	10:17	Scunthorpe Trent TC	Eastleigh Yard	18:47
6042	11:31	Halewood	Southampton E D	20:05

6M66 : On 10th April, DBS Class 66/0 No.66174 (above) passes Bourton, east of Swindon, with the diverted 09:32 Southampton Western Docks - Garston and a consist of imported Ford vehicles. The rake is a mix of 'IFA' (4908s), 'IPA' (4333s), 'IFA' (4376s) and 'IPA' (4333s), respectively.   **Martin Buck**

(Overleaf)

Page 34 : 6B33 : A superb choice of location .... Class 60 No.60091 is passing the weir at Greenland Mill on the approach to Bradford-on-Avon with the diverted 6B33, 11:11 Theale Murco - Margam TC empty petroleum bogie tanks. The first wagon is an internationally registered 'TIA' (7899) bogie tank.

Page 35 : 4V62 : The diverted 6V62, 10:44 Tilbury Riverside - Llanwern steel train, headed by Colas Class 60 No.60076, makes for a fine sight, as it travels alongside the Kennet & Avon Canal at Crofton on 8th April. The Canal runs from Bristol to Reading and the summit is at Crofton (450 feet above sea level), where a pumping station, complete with two beam engines, was erected to pump the water from natural springs in the area to the summit.   **Mark Pike (2)**

End of an Era

Background

The Shell oil terminal at Jarrow (South Tyneside) started to receive petroleum from Lindsey oil refinery (South Humberside) in 1998, following a successful trial; Class 56 No.56133 worked the first train to the terminal on 15th August 1997, running as 6Z41, the 13:02 Lindsey - Jarrow. Regular flows started running in 1998.

Last Train

Jarrow oil terminal cease taking railborne deliveries of petroleum, switching to pipeline and coastal shipping instead. The last train runs on Tuesday, 17th February, consisting of a mere 13 'TEA' bogie tanks, hauled by DBS Class 66/0 No.66055, in place of the usual Class 60.

6N03, 01:13 Lindsey - Jarrow	**6D43**, 16:20 Jarrow - Lindsey

In its heyday, Jarrow would receive up to 10 trains of petroleum per week, including supplies from Humber refinery; a normal consist would be 27 'TDA' / 'TEA' bogie tanks.

Previous Flows

Prior to this, the Stanlow refinery at Ellesmere Port supplied Jarrow with petroleum, transported in 2-axle 'TTA' tank wagons, until 1997 when Shell ceased all supplies by rail:

6E48, 04:49 (MO) Stanlow - Jarrow	Wigan Class 60
6E48, 07:09 (MSX) Stanlow - Jarrow	Wigan Class 60
6E15, 07:15 (MX) Stanlow - Jarrow	Wigan Class 60

Interestingly, both the loaded service and returning empties were routed via WCML (Shap) and the Tyne Valley (Hexham). At the time, these were the only petroleum tanks to run over the northern stretch of the WCML between Preston and Carlisle.

In the 1980s, prior to freight sectorisation, these trains were routed via the Calder Valley (Hebden Bridge) and ECML (York) using a combination of 2-axle and bogie tank wagons.

Portfolio

To mark the passing of the 'Jarrow Tanks', there now follows a small selection of images, illustrating the trains from both Lindsey and Stanlow.

(above): The 'Jarrow Tanks', just like most petroleum trains, attract Class 60 traction most of the time, although a DBS Class 66/0 will substitute from time to time. Here, on 3rd June 2010, Class 60 No.60010 in EWS maroon & gold livery passes Joan Croft Junction, slowing to leave the ECML and on to a 'freight only' line to join the Doncaster - Cleethorpes main line at Stainforth Junction.   **Alan Padley**

(opposite) : On reflection, the 'Jarrow Tanks' will be a sad omission from the working timetable, the only train 'booked' for Class 60 traction over the northern section of the ECML! On 16th April 2002, Transrail No.60058 'John Howard' heads alongside the Stainforth & Keadby Canal at Crowle. The canal connects the River Don Navigation at Bramwith to the River Trent at Keadby. It opened in 1802.   **Neil Harvey**

6N04 : "Early one morning, just as the sun was rising", Class 60 No.60038 'AvestaPolarit' (top left) approaches a frosty Barnetby on 12th December 2008 with 6N04, the 08:01 Lindsey - Jarrow loaded petroleum tanks.

The name 'AvestaPolarit' represents one of the largest producers of stainless steel, based in Sweden, formed in 2001 from a merger between Avesta Sheffield and Outokumpu. **Alan Padley**

6D43 : Class 60 No.60011 (middle) passes Pelaw on 21st February 2012 with 6D43, the 14:41 Jarrow - Lindsey empty bogie tanks. Behind the footbridge is Pelaw Junctions, where lines to Jarrow oil refinery and Leamside leave the Newcastle - Sunderland main line. **Martin Cook**

6N04 : Journey's end .... TATA Steel Livery No.60099 (below) sits in the winter sunshine at Jarrow Oil Terminal on 15th December 2011 for the tanks (off 6N04) to be emptied before setting off back to Humberside with 6D43 to Lindsey. The oil terminal is at the end of a single line, just over three miles from Pelaw Junction. **Martin Cook**

6N04 : 60073 (above), minus its 'Cairn Gorm' nameplates, approaches Colton Junction with a lengthy rake of loaded petroleum bogie tanks, forming 6N04, the 08:01 Lindsey - Jarrow. Note the EWS 'Beasties' logo on the body side.

20th October 2010. **Neil Harvey**

6D43 : It's the returning empties from Jarrow which attract the greater photographic attention.

On a dreary 20th July 2010, Mainline blue liveried No.60011 (middle) snakes across the pointwork at Stainforth Junction with 6D43, the 13:50 Jarrow - Lindsey. **Alan Padley**

6D43 : 'Tanking' along close to its maximum permitted speed of 60mph, 'tug' No.60015 'Bow Fell' (right) is about to pass over Balne level crossing on 27th April 2011 with 6D43, the 14:02 Jarrow - Lindsey empty tanks.

The loco is passing Milepost 166, the cumulative mileage at this point between London King's Cross and Newcastle. **James Skoyles**

37888 'Petrolea' (above) looks impressive as it passes through the Calder Valley on 21st September 1989 at Mytholmroyd with 6M19, Jarrow - Stanlow empty 2-axle petroleum tanks. The loco was renumbered from No.37135 in December 1987, named 'Petroled' at Stratford TMD in May 1988 and allocated to the FPFS Pool (Railfreight Petroleum Stratford) on 10th September 1989.

A burnished looking No.60018 (below) is seen heading north at Beck Foot on the WCML (28th May 1997) with 6E48, the 07:09 Stanlow - Jarrow loaded 2-axle petroleum tanks. This loco was previously named 'Moel Siabod' from new until May 1997, when it was repainted in EWS Maroon & Gold livery.

47194 **'Bullidae'** (above) passes a semaphore signal just east of Hebden Bridge while at the head of 6E18, the 07:56 Stanlow - Jarrow on 25th April 1989 formed, on this occasion, of bogie petroleum tanks; the semaphore has since been replaced by a colour light.

This particular Class 47 loco was one of a batch that carried the names of Latin Shells. Each nameplate also carried the logo of the Shell Oil Company and, amongst other duties, these locos worked oil trains to and from the Shell refinery at Stanlow.

Taxonomically speaking, 'Bullidae' is classed as *Gastopoda Opisthobranchia,* of the *Cephalaspidea* order in the *Bulloidea* super family. I'm sure you really wanted to know that! **Neil Harvey (3)**

A super composition amidst stunning scenery. On 19th October 1996, Transrail No.60061 'Alexander Graham Bell' (above) is seen between Low Gill and Beck Foot on the WCML with a lengthy 6M19, the 11:12 Jarrow - Stanlow.   **Neil Harvey**

On 13th February 2012, No.60074 'Teenage Spirit' (above), adorned in Teenage Cancer Trust livery, shunts the loaded petroleum tanks from Lindsey (6N04) back into the oil terminal at Jarrow, high above the southern end of the Tyne Tunnel approach road. **Martin Cook**

Breaking More New Ground

Lindsey oil refinery, South Humberside, sees black, orange and yellow in earnest since the demise of *Loadhaul,* as Colas Rail develop their share of the petrochemical market by gaining three new flows out of the refinery.

Details of these flows are given below. They are, perhaps, not unsurprising gains from DBS, as these trains run on behalf of TOTAL, a French owned company, as is Colas Rail!

Details of the initial workings are:

Code	Train		Traction	Notes	
6M32	03:08 Lindsey - Preston Docks		60087	Bitumen	7th January
6V70	22:20 Lindsey - Colnbrook		60021	Aviation Fuel	3rd February
6M11	01:24 Lindsey - Rectory Junction		60002	Petroleum	3rd February

6M32	70.7790.025-0	70.7790.020-1	70.7790.029-2	70.7790.011-0	70.7790.000-3
	70.7790.004-5	70.7790.027-6	70.7790.002-9	70.7790.024-3	70.7790.013-6
	70.7790.006-0				

6V70	86926	86913	86927	86920	86916	86917	86923	86922	86925	86918
	86919	86911	86924	86910	78266	78222	78230	78250	78247	78264
	78272	78235	78205	78251	78206	78267	78277	78263	78211	78269

6M11	870298	870232	870287	870253	870249	870274	870339	870280	870295	870330
	870273	871001								
	85946	85974	85950	82207	85948	85963	85959	85965	82210	82205
	85972	86967								

Route Learning : Up to December 2014, the Colas livery has only been seen on a couple of occasions passing through the Calder Valley. However, with Colas taking over the operation of the Lindsey to Preston Docks bitumen flow at the beginning of January 2015 , the colours wil become a regular sight.

In preparation, driver route learning begins in December 2014, initially with a single Class 47, but sometimes a pair or a single Class 60. Starting from the Colas base in Doncaster, the loco works via the Calder Valley to Preston and during the first week of route learning, a crowded No.47727 'Rebecca' (above) crosses the River Calder at Mirfield on 3rd December 2014 heading for Preston. **Derek Holmes**

6E32 .... *"Lowryesque"* ....

Cornholme : The dark satanic mills and scenes of life in the industrial districts of North West England in the mid-20th century became the trademark of one of England's most famous artists - J. S. Lowry.

In this view, smoke billows from the chimney stack above Frosthulme Mill, as Colas 'tug' No.60076 (above) steadies the early running 6E32, 08:55 Preston Docks Lanfina - Lindsey empty bitumen tanks down the grade through Cornholme, on a wintry 19th January. Frosthulme Mill is still in use, albeit not for its original purpose.

Cornholme was historically a part of Lancashire and falls within the OL (Oldham) postcode area, but became part of the West Riding of Yorkshire on 1st January 1888.

David Hayes

On 4th March, the erstwhile 'Penyghent', No.60021 (above), passes Oakley (near Bedford) on the Midland Main Line (MML) with a full length train of discharged bogie tanks; 6E38, the 13:54 Colnbrook - Lindsey. Note, the first two bogie tanks, which are Tiphook 'TDAs', built by Marley International in 1990. **Nigel Gibbs**

6E38

Further north on the MML, on 20th May, No.60021 (below) is seen again hauling 6E38 discharged bogie tanks, passing the giant cooling towers at Ratcliffe power station, as FHH Class 66/5 No.66563 waits to join the main line with 4E57, the 19:18 Ratcliffe - Hunslet empty 'HYA' coal hoppers. **Jamie Squibbs**

6E82 The delivery has been completed and now No.60087 'CLIC Sargent' (above) prepares to leave the oil terminal with 6E82, the 12:16 Rectory Junction - Lindsey empty bogie tanks. The train will now run to Grantham, where it will reverse before continuing its journey back to Humberside. Interestingly, the loaded train runs to Beeston South Junction for a reversal, before retracing its steps and propelling the loaded tanks into the oil sidings. **Mick Tindall**

During a week's trial (w/c 27th July) to test the feasibility of using a Class 70 on petrochemical flows out of Lindsey oil refinery, No.70802 and 70806 are despatched to South Humberside. Here, having worked out on the loaded train (6M11), No.70806 (below) approaches Barnetby station with the returning empties, 6E82, the 12:16 Rectory Junction - Lindsey. **Duncan Scott**

Diversions & Re-timings

Hatfield & Stainforth : By the time this image was taken (9th July), Hatfield Mine had closed, coal production ceased and with it the loss of 400 jobs. No.60047 (below) is hauling 6V70, the 18:11 Lindsey - Colnbrook loaded fuel oil tanks. The train is being diverted via Scunthorpe and Doncaster due to a major derailment on 30th June near to the level crossing at Langworth, between Barnetby and Lincoln; 10 empty wagons from 6E54, Kingsbury - Humber (hauled by Class 60 No.60054) derailed, causing significant damage to the line, which remained closed for 10 days. **Stuart Chapman**

Lydgate : With 'Erica' sitting pretty on the hillside in the foreground, No.60095 (below) crawls across Lydgate Viaduct on 2nd September with 6M32, the 05:18 Lindsey - Preston Docks loaded bitumen tanks, retimed due to engineering works in the Scunthorpe area. The train normally leaves Lindsey two hours earlier and it's this retiming which makes this photograph possible. **Neil Harvey**

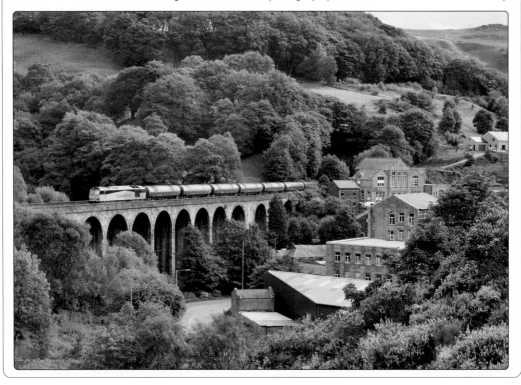

6E32

Location	Time	Location	Time
PRESTON DOCKS	09:30	Calder Bridge Jct.	11:36
Skew Bridge	09:48	Crofton West Jct.	11:38
Faringdon Curve Jct.	09:49	Hare Park Jct.	11:45
Lostock Hall	09:51	Fitzwilliam	11:48
BLACKBURN	10:22	South Elmsall	11:54
Accrington	10:30	Adwick Jct.	11:58
Rose Grove	10:37	Stainforth Jct.	12:09
Burnley Manchester Road	10:39	Hatfield & Stainforth	12:11
Hebden Bridge	10:57	Thorne South	12:14
Mytholmroyd	10:58	Crowle	12:21
Sowerby Bridge	11:03	Althorpe	12:27
Brighouse	11:10	SCUNTHORPE	12:33
Mirfield	11:14	Barnetby	12:50
Thornhill L.N.W. Jct.	11:16	Brocklesby Jct.	12:56
Healey Mills	11:23	Ulceby	12:58
WAKEFIELD KIRKGATE	11:35	LINDSEY OIL REFINERY	13:09

Stainforth East : The second Colas 'tug' to enter revenue-earning service is No.60076 (above), which is seen passing Hatfield Mine on 20th February, approaching Stainforth East, with 6E32, the 09:30 Preston Docks - Lindsey empty bitumen tanks. It's the returning empties which afford good photo opportunities, as the selective images show. **Alan Padley**

(Overleaf) :

Accrington : Colas 'tug' No.60076 (Page 50) catches a bit of sun as it rides the viaduct over the rooftops of Accrington, Lancashire, with 6E32 ex-Preston Docks discharged bitumen tanks. Accrington viaduct opened in 1847 for the East Lancashire Railway and is a curved structure of 19 (originally 21) semicircular brick arches, 40ft. in length and 60ft. high. **David Hayes**

Stainforth East : Here it comes .... on a gloomy 7th January, the first day of Colas operation, the odd splash of colour brightens up proceedings. No.60087 'CLIC Sargent' (Page 51) passes Hatfield Mine with 6E32, as an unidentified DBS Class 66/0 loco heads towards Doncaster with 6J94, the 12:25 Hull steel terminal - Rotherham, formed of bogie bolster wagons. **Alan Padley**

Cornholme : *"Potting the Yellow"* - No.60021 (above) makes a fleeting appearance across the factory rooftops of Cornholme in the Calder Valley, as it heads 6E32, the 09:30 Preston Docks - Lindsey. This is an unusual composition, well thought out, the interplay of all the angles is fascinating to study.   **David Hayes**

Thorne South : On 26th January, No.60021 (below) is seen in charge of 6E32 approaching Thorne South station and past the prominent water tower, which is one of two which supply Thorne. Boreholes were sunk at Dunsville in 1911 to provide water for Thorne and Hatfield, prior to which there had been only two deep boreholes, one supplying the brewery, the other the workhouse!   **Alan Padley**

South Elmsall : No.60087 *'CLIC Sargent'* (above) is seen on 13th February, heading 6E32 through South Elmsall station. This service only runs 'under the wires' between Preston South Jct. and Farington Curve Jct. (1.5 miles) and on the ECML between Hare Park Jct. and Adwick Jct. (11.75 miles).   **Alan Padley**

Horbury : Four days earlier, No.60087 (below) passes Horbury Bridge in glorious sunshine. Two yard lights stand tall in the former Healey Mills marshalling yard. Healey Mills lost its allocation of locos in 1984 and the marshalling yards closed in 1987, although still used for stabling locos and trains until the early 2000s. The driver depot closed from 4th February 2012, relocating to Wakefield Kirkgate.   **Pauline McKenna**

"Dalston tanks go Orange": From October, the Grangemouth - Dalston petroleum tanks (6M34 Loaded / 6S36 Empties) go over to Colas Rail operation and Class 60 traction. Here, on the first of the month, the first run of the northbound 6S36, 08:32 Dalston - *Grangemouth* empty bogie tanks is seen headed by No.60056 (above) crossing the infant River Clyde at Crawford. The train is formed mainly of VTG 'TEA' bogie tanks.   **Alastair Blackwood**

Nos.68007 'Valiant' + 68004 'Rapid' (above) climb through the Lune Gorge at Borrowbridge, on 7th February with 4S43, the 06:16 Daventry - Mossend intermodal. At this point, the WCML, the M6 Motorway, A6 road and the River Lune all squeeze through the Lune Gorge between Tebay Fell and Grayrigg. The southbound, off-side, crash barrier of the M6 Motorway is partially visible. **Fred Kerr**

Spreading Their Wings

The DRS Class 68s were built during 2014 by Vossloh España in Valencia, Spain, for use on both passenger and freight trains, numbered 68001 - 68015.

DRS have ordered 10 more!

The Class are now finding regular work ....

Freight : Intermodal, Departmental & Infrastructure services.

Passenger : London Marylebone - Birmingham Moor Street diagrams.
Edinburgh Waverley "Fife Circle" commuter trains.

Anglo-Scottish Intermodal

In early 2015, DRS Class 68s start working Anglo-Scottish intermodal services out of Daventry.

4S43 : On 13th February, No.68003 'Astute' (top) passes Balshaw Lane Junction, heading 4S43, the 06:16 Daventry - Mossend 'Tesco Express' intermodal single-handed; a service which would soon become 'booked' for a pair of Class 68s to ensure good timekeeping!

4S44 : On 7th January, the second of three daily northbound DRS intermodal services (the third being 4S45) passes Winwick, in the outskirts of Warrington, headed by No.68007 'Valiant' (above); the train is the 12:13hrs Daventry - Coatbridge.   **Fred Kerr (2)**

4S43

4S43, the 'Tesco Express' is a big train, as can be seen as it snakes through the long reverse curve on the approach to Rugeley Trent Valley, with Nos. 68002 'Intrepid' + 68003 'Astute' (above) in charge, on a dull 25th March. Ultimately, double-heading doesn't last, the call of other duties result in the 68s being replaced on the 'Tesco Express' by pairs of DRS Class 66s.   **John Whitehouse**

This powerful image also shows Nos.68002 'Intrepid' + 68003 'Astute' (below), but this time storming through a rainy Acton Bridge on 19th February at the head of 4S43. The fore-shortening affect of a telephoto lens, the lamp posts and catenary supports help create a powerful vista.   **David Hayes**

Banbury : On 2nd July, 1K65, the 18:47 London Marylebone - Kidderminster approaches Banbury station. No.**68012** (above) passes semaphore signals No.BS27 and No.BS33 , installed only a couple of years ago to help manage FGW trains diverted via Banbury to and from London Paddington. The GWR south box, along with Banbury North box, still survive, but both will be decommissioned in the near future.

Chiltern Moves

Kings Sutton : On the same day, but viewed from a public foot crossing, just north of Kings Sutton railway station, No.**68013** (above) approaches MAS colour light signal No.BS108 with 1K62, the 18:15 London Marylebone - Kidderminster, running some 10 minutes late.   **Nick Slocombe (2)**

London Marylebone

No.**68012** (right) is waiting to depart Platform 3 with the last northbound loco-hauled train of the day; 1K65, to Kidderminster.

(19th June) **Pauline McKenna**

Daytime loco-hauled trains out of Marylebone are:

1R15 : Birmingham Moor St.

1R22 : Birmingham Moor St.

1G25 : Birmingham Snow Hill

1R37 : Birmingham Moor St.

1R55 : Birmingham Moor St.

1K57 : Kidderminster

1U61 : Banbury

1K62 : Kidderminster

1K65 : Kidderminster

(Overleaf)

Leamington Spa : "Manicured". This station probably ranks as one of the most well kept stations on the network with superb flower beds and the retention of many GWR features. Class 68 No.**68013** (page 60) slows for the station stop on 23rd June with 1R37, the 13:15 London Marylebone - Birmingham Moor Street.

Birmingham Snow Hill : A complete contrast. Within the surrounds of the second city's metropolis, modern buildings overshadow No.**68013** (Page 61), as it awaits departure time from Birmingham Snow Hill with train 1H55, the 13:12hrs service to London Marylebone.

Snow Hill was once the main station of the Great Western Railway in Birmingham, in its heyday rivalling New Street station, with services to London Paddington, Wolverhampton Low Level and Birkenhead Woodside. Electrification of the main line from London to New Street in the 1960s spelled the end for Snow Hill, resulting in most of its services being withdrawn, leading to the station's eventual closure in 1972. Snow Hill station was revived and a new rebuilt station opened in 1987. **Colin Partington (2)**

Kilburn : It's a close shave, but a photograph is managed before a Stanmore bound Jubilee Line train (1996 Stock / No.**96060**) masks the view of No.**68012** (above) heading north on 18th June with 1K62, the 18:15hrs service from London Marylebone to Kidderminster. **Nick Slocombe**

The 'Banbury' Set

Kings Sutton : A 'classic' setting .... No.**68015** (above) approaches Banbury Lane road bridge, just north of Kings Sutton station, on 2nd July with 1U61, the 17:50 London Marylebone - Banbury, formed of the iconic InterCity blue/grey 'slam door' Mk3 set. These ex-Cargo D coaches were originally used by Wrexham, Shropshire and Marylebone Railway when loco-hauled services were introduced in 2008.   **Nick Slocombe**

Hadenham & Thame Parkway : The first significant snowfall in this area during the Winter was overnight from 2nd to 3rd February, though nothing like as heavy as other areas. Chiltern DVT No.82302 leads the blue/grey slam door Mk3 'Banbury Set' into Hadenham & Thame Parkway station with No.**68015** (below) propelling on its passenger debut. The train is 1H20, the 07:44 Banbury - London Marylebone and, unusually, 1H20 operated with No.67010 and a silver set of coaches the previous day!   **Geoff Plumb**

Princes Risborough : Taking a break from its normal duties on 30th May, No.**68013** (above) is hard on the heels of No.68014 whilst working another FA Cup Final extra. This is 5R52 ECS from Wembley LMD to Birmingham Moor Street, where it will form 1I50, the 12:25 from Moor Street to Wembley Stadium. The "Banbury" set is not normally in use at weekends or north of Banbury.   **Geoff Plumb**

Kings Sutton : A variation on a theme and a close up view of DRS Compass liveried No.68009 'Titan' (below), fast approaching on 12th August with 1U61, the 17:50 London Marylebone - Banbury. Of note is the 14th century church of St Peter and St Paul. The spire reaches a height of 198ft and is one of the finest in Northamptonshire, according to Sir Nikolaus Bernhard Leon Pevsner (1902 – 1983), a scholar, best known for his 46-volume series of county-by-county guides, "The Buildings of England (1951–74)".   **Nick Slocombe**

Hatton Bank : On 11th May, No.**68014** (above) is seen accelerating up Hatton Bank on 11th May with 1R55, the 16:47 London Marylebone - Birmingham Moor Street and, unusually for a Chiltern Railways train, it is running 19 minutes late.

The train is running alongside the 'Down Goods' loop, which starts at Bugbrooke (Milepost 110.79) and ends 1 mile and 132 yards later, just south of Hatton station. From Warwick Parkway, the line climbs at a steady ruling gradient of 1 in 107 for nearly four miles, before reaching Hatton. **Martin Loader**

Birmingham Moor Street : Journey's end and a station absolutely brimming with Great Western Railway architecture. Class 68 No.**68013** (bottom left) stands at the blocks on 23rd June, having arrived with 1R37, the 13:15 London Marylebone -Birmingham Moor Street. After servicing, the train set will return south as 1H69, the 15:55 Birmingham Moor Street - London Marylebone.

Leamington Spa : No.**68013** (top left) is seen again, 30 minutes after leaving Birmingham, on the rear of 1H69, as it passes under the station clock, making its way out of Leamington Spa, propelling all the way to London. These Chiltern 'Silver Services' are an absolute delight to travel, with comfort and quality and four seats around a table by a window - a standard to which all TOCs should conform!

Colin Partington (2)

"The Fife Circle"

Background History : In February, it is announced that DBS will cease operating the morning and evening rush-hour commuter trains between Edinburgh Waverley - Cardenden - Glenrothes with Thornton - Edinburgh Waverley.

DRS will take over the duties relinquished by DBS Class 67s from April.

Traction : Class 68s.

Loco Diagrams

Diagram 1

5K18,	05:11	Motherwell TMD - Cardenden	via Falkirk Grahamston & Kirkcaldy
2K18,	07:35	**Cardenden - Edinburgh Waverley**	via Dunfermline
5K19,	08:47	Edinburgh Waverley - Motherwell TMD	via 'Suburban Line' & Shotts
5G13,	14:54	Motherwell TMD - Edinburgh Waverley	via Shotts & 'Suburban Line'
2G13,	17:08	**Edinburgh Waverley - Glenrothes with Thornton**	via Dunfermline
2K14,	18:15	**Glenrothes with Thornton - Edinburgh Waverley**	via Kirkcaldy
5K14,	19:47	Edinburgh Waverley - Motherwell TMD	via 'Suburban Line' & Shotts

Diagram 2

5L69,	16:03	Motherwell TMD - Edinburgh Waverley	via Shotts & 'Suburban line'
2L69,	17:20	**Edinburgh Waverley - Cardenden**	via Dunfermline
5L70,	18:24	Cardenden - Motherwell TMD	via Kirkcaldy & Falkirk Grahamston

(Above) : On 27th February, DRS commence Fife Circle crew training runs in lieu of their new loco haul duties, on behalf of ScotRail. Class 68 No.68004 'Rapid' passes Lathallan, near Polmont, with a 5Z69, Motherwell - Fife - Motherwell, formed of coaching stock numbered (from front to back) 3345, 3344, 3325, 3333, 3390 and 9527. **Guy Houston**

(Opposite) : Having just exited North Queensferry tunnel, ScotRail liveried No.68006 'Daring' rounds the curve past Ferryhills on 9th April, while working 2L69, the 17:20 Edinburgh - Cardenden ScotRail Fife Circle service. The gorse has grown so much here now, that this was the best possible angle without starting to lose the side of the loco behind the foreground bushes. **Steven Brykajlo**

Fife Circle

Jamestown (Fife) : On the first day of DRS operation on the *'Fife Circle'* , Class 68 No.68006 'Daring' (above) is seen in charge of 2K18, the 07:35 Cardenden - Edinburgh, formed of Scotrail branded Mk2 vehicles Nos.5965, 5976, 6176, 9539, 6177 and 6183. The train has just crossed Jamestown Viaduct, close to where the railway skirts the A90.

Jamestown Viaduct is part of the northern approach to the Forth Bridge. Constructed between 1887 and 1890, it has four main steel girder spans, supported by three sandstone piers. The steel spans are 110 ft long and are at a skew of 70°. **Guy Houston**

Here, this time on 16th April, No.68007 'Valiant' (below) is viewed from the other side of the line having crossed Jamestown Viaduct with 2K14, the 18.15 Glenrothes - Edinburgh. The yellow gorse in the foreground nicely complements the shades of blue in the train. **Steven Brykajlo**

No.68004 'Rapid' (right) is coming off the Edinburgh 'Suburban' Line on 10th April and approaching Brunstane with 5G13, the 14:54 Motherwell - Edinburgh Waverley ECS.

Note the bridge piers, which once carried the line from Portobello to Walton Walls Jct, joining the ECML at Monktonhall Jct.

Routed via Shotts & the 'Suburban' line, No.68006 'Daring' (below) is now at Niddrie West Junction with the points set for the train (5G13, 14:54 Motherwell TMD - Edinburgh Waverley) to go via Brunstane to Portobello Junction.

At Portobello, the ECS will wait around 30 minutes, before going into Waverley, to form 2G13 to Glenrothes with Thornton.

Keith McGovern (2)

(Overleaf) :

68003 'Astute' (Page 70) passes Burntisland Links golf course on the evening of 21st April, while working 5L70, Cardenden - Motherwell ECS, after working 2L69 ex-Edinburgh Waverley.

68006 'Daring' (Page 71) is nearing its destination, as it passes through the famous Princes Street Gardens on 11th May with 2K18, the 07:35 Cardenden - Edinburgh.   **Steven Brykajlo (2)**

This is a view from a new pedestrian footbridge installed in the Esplanade area of Dundee. No.68007 'Valiant' and No.68006 'Daring' (above, respectively) each head a rake of stock in the West Sidings, destined for Leuchars. Extra 'Golflink' services have been laid on for the convenience of spectators attending the 144th Open Golf Championship at St Andrews. In the background, an unidentified HST waits to leave Dundee Tay Bridge station with 1S03, the 07:10 Leeds - Aberdeen and note the masts of RRS. 'Discovery', the ship in which Captain Robert Falcon Scott set sail in 1901 to Antarctica.
Jim Ramsay

No.68003 'Astute' (below) approaches Healey Mills on Sunday, 7th June, with 5Z76, Cleethorpes - Crewe Northern Belle ECS, becoming the first 68 to haul a train through the Calder Valley. The train is returning to Crewe after working two Humberside based excursions during the weekend. The ECS was due through Healey Mills at 21:16hrs, only minutes before sunset. Fortunately, with a clear sky and the train running a minute early, the last of the low sun is shining under the bridge and illuminates No.68003, before sinking below the horizon minutes later.
Derek Holmes

Basingstoke : On 27th March, No.68009 'Titan' (above) passes Battledown Flyover (three miles west of Basingstoke) running light from Crewe to Eastleigh (0Z70) to collect some refurbished Mk2f coaches, for use on the DRS operated 'Fife Circle' commuter trains. Whilst images of a light engine move do not tick everybody's boxes, a Class 68 on the Southern is not, and may not become, an everyday occurrence, so is worth recording for posterity. **Simon Howard**

Dundee : On 19th July, in abysmal conditions, No.68001 'Evolution' (below) brings up the rear of 5Z80, Dundee - Leuchars 'Golflink' ECS; No.68007 is the train loco leading. The train is making its way from Dundee up the incline (ruling gradient of 1 in 70) towards the Tay Railway Bridge; the elevation clearly discernible in this image.

The present Tay Bridge is the second one on the site. The first, opening in 1878, suddenly collapsed in a high wind on 28 December 1879, resulting in one of the great engineering disasters of history. The second (present) structure spanning the Firth of Tay opened in 1887 and is 2.75 miles long. **Jim Ramsay**

Hatfield & Stainforth : No.68001 'Evolution' (above) breaks new ground on 17th March, believed to be the first Class 68 on the Doncaster - Cleethorpes main line. It's approaching Hatfield & Stainforth with a special 6Z52, Toton - Scunthorpe empty welded rail train, as an unidentified DBS Class 66/0 waits to come off the 'Up Skellow' 'freight only' line with a rake of empty 'HTA' coal hoppers.   **Alan Padley**

Chellaston : On 9th April, one of the locos subcontracted to Chiltern Trains to work passenger services on the London Marylebone - Banbury - Birmingham Moor Street - Kidderminster - Stourbridge Junction route, No.**68011** (below), is surprisingly seen passing Chellaston with a special 6Z44, Bescot - Toton engineer's 'trip'. The consist is a rake of track panel carrying wagons conveying concrete sleepers and Chellaston is on the Stenson Junction - Sheet Stores 'freight only' line.   **Jamie Squibbs**

Allandale : No.68006 'Daring' (above) powers north near Blackford on 8th December 2014 with 4A13, the 12:20 Grangemouth - Aberdeen intermodal. The snow covered peaks of the Scottish Southern Highlands form the backdrop; Ben More, standing at 3,851ft, is prominent in the view.   **Alastair Blackwood**

Beattock

On 21st April, dropping down Beattock in glorious sunshine, No.68004 'Rapid' (top left) passes Greskine with two coaches in tow, running as 5Z44, Motherwell - Derby. Meanwhile, 68007 'Valiant' (bottom left) is seen climbing through Greskine on 5th November 2014 with a 4Z40, Carlisle Kingmoor - Rutherglen wagon move.

The WCML climbs for 10 miles from Beattock to Beattock Summit at a ruling gradient of 1 in 77. For northbound trains, the climb is more arduous and, in the halcyon days of steam, some trains would call upon the 'Beattock Bankers' to get up the bank, which were on standby 24-hours a day.

Greskine is the mid-way point on the climb to Beattock Summit and, prior to colour light signalling, a signal box was located just north of this point.   **Keith McGovern (2)**

Carnoustie : On 30th July, a ScotRail liveried Class 68 loco finds itself away from its normal 'Fife Circle' commuter diagrams, working 4A13, the 12:20 Grangemouth - Aberdeen intermodal and 4N83 18:20hrs return. On a glorious summer evening, No.68006 'Daring' (below) powers south through Carnoustie with a well loaded 4N83, Aberdeen Craiginches - Grangemouth.   **Jim Ramsay**

Breaking New Ground

Background History

By the end of May 2014, all 10 Colas Class 70s had arrived in the UK and were available for work. The last one, No.70810, arrived at Liverpool's Seaforth Dock on 26th May having crossed the Atlantic Ocean onboard the ACL vessel MV 'Atlantic Concert'.

The Class was initially employed on engineer's and infrastructure trains working out of Eastleigh and Westbury, which still remains the case today.

What's New

However, new duties have followed, such as coal and timber, plus continuing departmental and infrastructure trains on behalf of Network Rail to pastures new.

COAL

Colas 70s share coal diagrams with the Colas 66s, moving imported coal from Avonmouth and Portbury Dock to Aberthaw and Ratcliffe power station, respectively.

No.70809 (left) passes Willington on the Derby - Birmingham main line with 4V12 coal empties, ex-Ratcliffe ps, running to Gloucester New Yard, where they will be staged, prior to a trip to the docks for another consignment of the black stuff.
Alan Padley

4C30 : Colas start running to Aberthaw power station in December 2014, when No.70803 has the honour of hauling the first train. In this view, No.70803 (above) is seen between Rhoose and Barry, crossing Porthkerry Viaduct with 4C30, the 08:58 (MO) Aberthaw PS - Gloucester New Yard coal empties. The viaduct is 376 yards long and was constructed between 1896 - 1899.
Chris Davies

4C30 : Here, No.70803 (above) is seen again (2nd February) approaching Cadoxton on the Vale of Glamorgan Line with 4C30, 08:58 (MO) Aberthaw PS - Gloucester New Yard coal empties.

The lower line in the foreground leads from Barry Docks Line Junction to Barry Docks and is used ostensibly for chemical traffic to and from the Dow Corning Chemicals plant. There is a daily wagonload 'trip' between Newport Alexandra Dock Junction and Barry Docks (6B06 / 6B39) for this purpose.   **Chris Davies**

4V12 : No.70809 (below) is passing Whitacre Junction with 4V12, the 09:00 Ratcliffe power station - Gloucester New yard coal empties. The train has arrived here after leaving the Derby - Birmingham main line at Kingsbury Junction. The line to Nuneaton is to the right.   **Pauline McKenna**

TIMBER Interspersed between Class 56s and latterly Class 60s, Colas 70s start working timber trains to Chirk. On the first day of Class 70 traction (25th March), the northbound train from Teigngrace to Chirk (6M51), is headed by No.70804 (above) and is seen passing alongside the sea wall on the approach to Dawlish Warren, running late at the time. **Robert Sherwood**

Normally scheduled to run on Tuesday and Thursday, No.70804 (below) is seen again, this time running through Walterstone Common on Wednesday, 8th April, working 6M51, the 15:25 Baglan Bay - Chirk loaded timber train. The distinctive Skirrid Hill is in the background and the River Monnow courses close to the railway here, which is between Llanvighangel and Pontrilas. **Chris Davies**

PETR0 - CHEMICALS

Week commencing 27th July, Colas try out their Class 70s on petrochemical flows out of Lindsey oil refinery to Colnbrook, Preston Docks and Rectory Junction (Nottingham), using Nos.70802 and 70806.

Having crossed Horsfall Viaduct, No.70802 (above) approaches Horsfall Tunnel on the Calder Valley main Line with 6E32, the 08:55 Preston Docks - Lindsey empty bitumen tanks. This is the first time a Class 70 has worked this particular train.

Neil Harvey

ECML : Weekend engineering work over 11th and 12th October 2014, sees the closure of the Scottish section of the ECML.

One of the work sites was just west of Oxwellmains Cement Works and a total of 6 engineers' trains worked here from Tyne Yard. The last one (6K14) was worked top 'n' tail by two Colas Class 70s.

Here, No.70806 (top right) brings up the rear of 6K14, standing adjacent to the cement works on Saturday, the 11th. **Keith McGovern**

A new location for a Class 70 (unless anyone knows to the contrary) sees No.70803 (bottom right) at London King's Cross on 7th December 2014 with a civil engineer's duty. This is on 6C51, the 01:50 Belle Isle - Whitemoor and No.70810 was on the north end of the train.

The engineer's have possession of four platforms due to work in the Belle Isle / Holloway area and DBS 'sheds', Nos.66084, 66043, 66116 and 66145 were also present.

Grand Central HST power car No.43467 is on the rear of 1N96, the 18:54hrs service to Sunderland, standing at Platform 4. **Nigel Gibbs**

SYSTON & PETERBOROUGH RAILWAY : This former railway is now part of the Cross Country route which links Birmingham and Peterborough.

On 11th April, No.70806 (above) is seen hauling Plasser & Theurer 09-3X 'tamper' No.DR73117 past Uffington, Lincolnshire, on 6Z12, the 11:15 Norwich - Rugby. Network Rail use the Mid-Norfolk Railway to store OTP (On Track Plant) vehicles, from where this 'tamper' originated. **Nigel Gibbs**

PAIGNTON : No.70804 (below) pulls into Paignton with 'Railvac' No.99709515003-0 in tow, running as 6C51, the 09:13 Westbury Down TC - Goodrington Carriage Sidings on Thursday, 22nd January, waiting for permission to proceed. This is the first visit of a Colas 70 to the Paignton branch. **Robert Sherwood**

Engineering 'Trips'

The Self-Discharge Train (SDT) is Redland's greatest rail freight innovation; introduced in 1988, it consists of hopper wagons linked by an on-board conveyor belt, which feeds a 'KJA' discharge wagon. The SDT works out of Mountsorrel and is used to supply aggregate where no discharge facilities exist.

No.70808 (above) provides a rare sight of a Colas Class 70 on the SDT, seen on 28th March at work between Plumstead and Abbey Wood off-loading ballast for the Crossrail project. **Ian Cuthbertson**

> **Self Discharge Train**

Meanwhile, its job done, and a return to base. No.70808 (below) passes Oakley, near Bedford, on the 'Down Slow' line with 6C60, the 13.25 Slade Green - Mountsorrel. Class 70s are not an everyday sight on the Midland Main Line. **Nigel Gibbs**

CHESHIRE & SHROPSHIRE

Unless the Chirk 'logs' is Class 70 hauled, the rails in this part of northern England will probably not reverberate to Colas 'Powerhaul' traction, unless working civil engineer's 'trips', as illustrated here.

Colas Class 70 No.70802 (above) leaves Chester with a rake of 20 (4 sets) loaded autoballasters, bound for Wrexham. It is crossing the Dee Viaduct, designed by Robert Stephenson for the Chester and Holyhead Railway, opening in 1846. In the early 1900s, it was widened to four tracks but later reduced to two tracks.

A wide angle lens helps bring more into the frame, such as 'Roodee', better known as Chester racecourse, the oldest in the country, along with a Class 175 DMU on a passenger service from Holyhead. **Alan Hazelden**

Meanwhile, the low suns glints off the side of 6C21, the 05:55 East Usk - Crewe ballast empties, as the driver of No.70806 (below) negotiates his train through the reverse curves at Hadnall. What's left of the former station buildings can be seen directly above the last wagon. **Mike Hemming**

25th Anniversary

Background : The British Rail Class 90 electric locos were built by BREL at Crewe between 1987 - 1990, each weighing 84.5 tonnes with a top speed of 110 mph, operated from 25 kV AC overhead lines. 2015 represents the ***25th anniversary of the last Class 90 built.***

The Class 90s are now deployed on Abellio Greater Anglia passenger services from London Liverpool Street to Norwich and freight operations for DB Schenker and Freightliner on a mixture of roles, mainly on the West Coast Main Line and the Great Eastern Main Line.

Description : Fifty Class 90/0 locos (numbered 90001 - 90050) were originally developed from the Class 87, built primarily to replace 1960s-built Class 81, 82, 83, 84 and 85 electric locos.

Initial Distribution

90001 - 90015 : *InterCity* express passenger services.

90016 - 90020 : repainted into the new Rail Express Systems (ReS) livery and dedicated to mail trains, principally London - Glasgow and London - Newcastle services.

90021 - 90024 : Railfreight Distribution, but available to cover InterCity failures.

90025 - 90050 : Under sectorisation, 26 locos dedicated for freight traffic.

The latter group of locos were reclassified Class 90/1 and renumbered 90125 - 90150 by the addition of 100 to the original number. This resulted in the maximum speed reducing to 75 mph.

Some of the locos received the new Railfreight Distribution two-tone grey livery and three (Nos.90128, 90129 and 90130), received a special 'continental' livery, NMBS/SNCB blue, DB red and SNCF grey, respectively to celebrate '*Freightconnection*' in 1992.

Names : Some Class 90s were named, but not all. The passenger locos were named after cities, newspapers or famous institutions and the Class 90 became the first new loco to carry the *InterCity* Swallow livery. Freight locos had names with a commercial link.

State of Play at 3rd January 2015

ABELIO GREATER ANGLIA

90001 - 90015   Liverpool Street - Norwich turns

D B SCHENKER

90017	Stored	90018	Crewe IEMD
90019	Scotrail Sleeper Use	90020	ScotRail Sleeper Use
90021	Crewe IEMD	90022	Stored
90023	Stored	90024	ScotRail Sleeper Use
90025	Stored	90026	ScotRail Sleeper Use
90027	Stored	90028	Crewe IEMD
90029	Crewe IEMD	90030	Stored
90031	Stored	90032	Stored
90033	Stored	90034	Crewe IEMD
90035	Mossend Yard	90036	ScotRail Sleeper Use
90037	Scotrail Sleeper Use	90038	Stored
90039	Scotrail Sleeper Use	90040	Stored

FREIGHTLINER

90016	Crewe, Basford Hall	4F64, Crewe Basford Hall - Garston
90041	Crewe, Basford Hall	
90042	Crewe, Basford Hall	
90043	Crewe, Basford Hall	4L89, Crewe Basford Hall - Ipswich Yard
90044	Crewe, Basford Hall	
90045	Ipswich Yard	4M88, Felixstowe - Crewe Basford Hall
90046	Mossend Yard	4L81, Coatbridge - London Gateway
90047	Crewe, Basford Hall	
90048	Crewe, Basford Hall	
90049	Crewe, Basford Hall	4L41, Crewe Basford Hall - Ipswich Yard
90050	Stored	

Notes :

a) Nos.90019 / 90021 / 90024 are in First ScotRail livery.

b) Nos.90018 / 90029 / 90036 are in DB Schenker Red livery.

c) No.90034 now in DRS Blue livery.

d) No.90050 has been in store since catching fire in 2004.

No.90044 Builder's Plate   Syd Young

Class 90 Specifications

Configuration	:	Bo-Bo
Length	:	61ft. 8ins.
Height	:	13ft.
Weight	:	84.5 tonnes
Electrical System	:	25 kV AC Catenary
Traction Motors	:	GEC 1,250 hp (930 kW)
Power Output	:	5,000 bhp
Top Speed	:	110 mph
Tractive Effort	:	58,000 lbf

(Opposite) : *Under Construction* : **Crewe BREL Works** ; No.**90004** (nearest the camera) is in the final throes of construction and ready for a trip to the paint shop to be finished off, as is sister loco No.**90005**, which already sports InterCity livery. (circa late 1980s)   **Ian Cuthbertson**

Freightconnection 1992

90128 'Vrachtverbinding'

On 29th March 1996, No.90128 (top left) is seen double heading No.90130 'Fretconnection' through Warrington Bank Quay station with 4S73, 05:43 Wembley - Mossend intermodal.

No.90128 carries the blue and yellow colours of Belgian National Railways.

90129 'Frachtverbindungen'

Sporting German Federal Railways red livery, No.90129 (middle) hurries through South Kenton on 11th May 1996 with curtainside 'swapbodies', bound for Wembley.

This particular intermodal is either 4A13 (13:10hrs ex-Trafford Park) or 4M72 10:25hrs ex-Mossend).

Ian Cuthbertson (2)

90130 'Fretconnection'

'A touch of French', as No.90130 (below) accelerates past Winwick, three miles north of Warrington Bank Quay, on 28th June 1993 with 4S59, Southampton Millbrook – Coatbridge freightliner. **Neil Harvey**

Focus on Freight

90130 'Allerton TRS Depot' (above) ambles south at Docker on 1st June 1993 with a very lightly loaded 6M79, the 12:00, Mossend - Washwood Heath 'Connectrail' service, formed of two Cargowaggons; the Cumbrian fells form an impressive backdrop. This loco was one of the 26 to be reclassified Class 90/1, having previously been numbered 90030.   **Neil Harvey**

90044 (below) has arrived at Warrington with a trainload of steel coil from Mossend (ex-Ravenscraig steelworks) destined for South Wales, one of many such Anglo-Scottish steel trains to run until the steelworks near Motherwell closed in 1992. The Class 90 will come off and hand over to Class 37/9 No.37901 'Mirrlees Pioneer' for the remainder of the journey via 'The Marches Route'. 7th June 1990.   **Syd Young**

90018 (left), substituting for the 'booked' DBS Class 92, heads past Holytown on 7th February 2013 with 6S51, 12:16 Carlisle Yard - Mossend departmental, the loco fresh from overhaul and a new lick of paint.

This turn, along with the balancing 6M49 from Mossend, switched to GBRf traction (Class 92) in 2013.

Kenny Marrs

90032 (middle) in BR InterCity Mainline colours approaches Brock foot crossing on 29th June 1991 with 6M27, the 06:20 Larbert - Oakleigh, formed of 2-axle ICI soda ash tanks.

This is a 20 mile section of two running lines between Preston and Lancaster. **Fred Kerr**

90028 (below) is seen heading along the WCML, just south of Tring station on 26th July 2012 with a rake of empty cargowaggons, which form 6A42, 14:42 Daventry - Wembley.

This is the return working of 6B41, which brings in bottled mineral water from France. **Ian Cuthbertson**

90039 (above) heads 6L48, the 16:31 Garston - Dagenham car carriers through Acton Bridge on 19th March 2012, a service which has since switched to GBRf haulage. Acton Bridge station is a popular location amongst enthusiasts, especially for viewing southbound freight services in the afternoon, like this one.

Acton Bridge lies 14 miles north of Crewe and 10 miles south of Warrington Bank Quay and services running to and from Liverpool join the WCML at Weaver Junction, two miles north of here.   **David Hayes**

(Overleaf) :

90038 (Page 92) heads south at Winwick Junction, near Warrington, on 23rd March 1991 with 6M27, the 06:20 Larbert - Oakleigh soda ash, formed of 2-axle tank wagons. Sadly, this flow no longer runs and although Oakleigh is used in railway timetables to record this and similar trains, the works are actually in the town of Northwich, but many would not know where you meant if you mentioned it.

The production of soda ash ceased when Tata Chemicals Europe shut their factory at Winnington in Northwich in 2014 due to rising gas prices. The factory has produced the chemical for industries such as glass and soap-making since 1874.   **Neil Harvey**

90016 (Page 93) is seen running past the Oxford Canal at Ansty on 27th August 2010 with 4M81, the 07:30 Felixstowe - Crewe Basford Hall freightliner. Basford Hall is a 'hub' on the freightliner network where container trains are re-marshalled.   **Nick Slocombe**

90042 (left) works 4M88, the 08:49 Felixstowe - Crewe Basford Hall freightliner on 23rd June 2010 and is seen heading downgrade (1 in . 45) at Brantham. The majority of freightliners working 'under the wires' on the Great Eastern Main Line are Class 90 hauled.

Ian Cuthbertson

90045 (middle) is seen at Carlisle on 26th March 2011 in its original Freightliner livery of two tone grey with black cab doors and window surrounds, plus red triangle logo, .

The Class 90 is working 4M74, the 14:01 Coatbridge - Crewe Basford Hall 'liner, deputising for the usual 2 x Class 86/6s.   **Kenny Marrs**

90050 (below) passes Winwick on 26th March 2004, with No.90041, double-heading 4M27, the 05:00 Coatbridge - Crewe Basford Hall, which conveys aluminium ingots from Fort William.

Despite being built to be less susceptible to fire damage than the Class 81s - 85s, No.90050 did catch fire in September 2004, prompting its storage and stripping for spares.

Fred Kerr

Freightliner

90041 (right) was one of the first Freightliner Class 90s to receive the distinctive green livery.

Here it is seen passing through Rugeley Trent Valley on a fine summer day in July 2004 with a fully loaded 4M81, 10:44 Ipswich Yard - Trafford Park.

The loco came onto the train at Ipswich as the Felixstowe branch is not electrified. **Martin Buck**

90016 (middle) is seen stabled taking a breather in between duties on 9th October 2011 at Basford Hall Yard along with 90043 'Freightliner Coatbridge'.

This provides a good comparison between the first version of Freightliner green livery and the original two tone grey.

Basford Hall is where trains are re-marshalled with portions being attached / detached for local terminals at Seaforth, Ditton, Garston and Trafford Park.

Kenny Marrs

The 'Powerhaul' guise is green livery with yellow cabs, green and grey swirls at each end, plus Freightliner branding. No.90045 (above) is seen on 15th March 2012 heading along the WCML approaching Soulbury north west of Leighton Buzzard with 4M88, the 09:20 Felixstowe - Basford Hall. **Nigel Gibbs**

90002 (above) passes Dillicar in the Lune Gorge on 11th April 1992 with the 'Up' 'Clansman' (14:40hrs Edinburgh Waverley - London Euston) and at least the Class 90's original livery shows up well in these poor conditions. There is an interesting range of coaching stock in this train, from the blue & grey Mk1 BG at the head of the train, through to the three 'GUVs' (General Utility Vans) at the rear. At this time, passenger locos wore the BR InterCity 'Swallow' livery, comprising dark grey, white, red and white bands on the body side.   **Martin Loader**

90029 (below) approaches Manchester Piccadilly on 10th May 1989 at the end of its journey from London Euston with a rake of similarly liveried Mk3 vehicles. The Class 90s were dubbed 'Skodas' by enthusiasts, akin to the namesake motor car, apparently to reflect poor craftsmanship and reliability!   **Neil Harvey**

90007 'Lord Stamp' (top right) stands at Preston on 17th January 2002 at the head of 1S94, 18:33 London Euston - Glasgow Central, alongside Class 158 No.158805.

No.90007 is currently working on behalf of abellio greateranglia and in a different livery. **Neil Harvey**

90026 (middle) in EWS maroon & gold livery, awaits departure time at London Euston in the early evening of 4th September 2003 with an unidentified express.

Alongside is Class 87 No.87002 'Royal Sovereign', adorned in the purple colours of Porterbrook Leasing. **Nick Slocombe**

90002 'Mission Impossible' (below) brings up the rear of 1P53, the 07:55 London Euston - Manchester Piccadilly 'Manchester Pullman' as it passes through Levenshulme on its inaugural run on 10th March 1997. Although a 'going away' shot, this was the only possible way to get a picture of the loco in its then brand new livery. Virgin West Coast had taken over the franchise for the route the previous day. **Martin Loader**

**orth Berwick
'Skodas'

90027 'Allerton T&RS Depot Quality Approved' (above) has just departed from Prestonpans on 5th May 2005 with 2Y11, the 11:17 North Berwick - Edinburgh Waverley.

This was a bizarre operation in the Class 90 history; during 2004/2005, Scotrail hired in loco-hauled stock to work the Edinburgh to North Berwick route, replacing Class 322s which transferred to London. The loco-hauled stock comprised three sets of three standard Mk3s + DVT + EWS Class 90 and there were two daytime diagrams, with three during peak periods, which extended to/from Haymarket.

90021 (below) comes off the single line branch on 21st February 2005, approaching the junction at Drem with the 13:17hrs North Berwick - Edinburgh Waverley. The North Berwick branch runs for just over four miles from Drem Junction and the only station on the line is North Berwick itself.   **Chris Perkins (2**

GNER 'Skodas'

Between 1999 - 2003, GNER regularly hired in one or more Class 90s from EWS to haul a Mk4 set, covering a motive power shortage. They were usually put to work on the King's Cross - Leeds circuit hauling Bounds Green 225 train sets BN461 and/or BN462.

90030 'Fretconnection' (above) heads south over Walton Viaduct, Wakefield, on 12th October 1999 propelling 1A32, the 12:40 Leeds - King's Cross, viewed from the Walton to Crofton road.

Meanwhile, during weekend diversions off the ECML, Class 47/7 No.47786 'Roy Castle OBE' leads Class 90 No.90025 (below) 'DIT' on 30th April 2000 through Goose Hill at the head of the diverted 18:14hrs Leeds - King's Cross. The train is passing the former Welbeck spoil terminal. **Neil Harvey (2**

'Pretendolino'

Following the loss of a Class 390 Pendolino in the 2007 Grayrigg derailment, Virgin deployed a Mk3 set + DVT with a Class 90 hired from EWS. In 2008, Virgin decided to retain the Mk3 set (WB64, now nicknamed 'Pretendolino') and use it with a Class 90 hired from Freightliner on the Euston - Birmingham New Street / Crewe - Preston corridor until its withdrawal in October 2014.

90007 'The Institution of Civil Engineers' (above) passes Blisworth on 11th August 2009 hauling the 'Pretendolino' set, forming 1G27, the 14:43 London Euston - Birmingham New Street. Blisworth is on the two track section of the WCML between Roade and Rugby.   **Nigel Gibb**

90045 (below), resplendent in Freightliner 'Powerhaul' livery, stands at Birmingham International station on 5th January 2011 at the head of 1K39, the 18:43 (FO) London Euston - Crewe.   **David Weake**

Virgin signed a two year contract in December 2013 with DRS to provide a Class 90 loco for its Mk3 set and No.90034 became the dedicated loco, attached to the 'Pretendolino' and kept at Wembley. No.90034 is owned by DBS and hired by DRS. It makes its maiden outing for Virgin trains on 3rd April 2014, in a version of DRS livery, working 1G40, the 19.03 London Euston - Birmingham N. St.

'Skoda' 90034 (above) is seen taking a rest at London Euston station on 10th April 2014 after working in with B94, the 20:50hrs service from Birmingham New Street.

90034 (above) is seen on 24th October 2014 from the Great Brickhill Road overbridge, just outside the village of Soulbury (near Leighton Buzzard) propelling 5Z58, the 11:25 Rugby - Wembley ECS.

Virgin Trains operated their last 'Pretendolino' scheduled services between London Euston - Birmingham New Street - London Euston in October 2014 on the usual Thursday/Friday runs. During its hire period, a selection of DRS and Freightliner Class 90s could be seen working the 'Pretendolino' set. **Nigel Gibbs (2)**

Anglian Diversity

90008 (above) : The Great Eastern Main Line benefits from a half hourly loco-hauled service linking Norwich to London Liverpool Street - here is one such working, 1P23, the 09:00 Norwich - London Liverpool Street service which is illustrated passing through the Essex countryside near Kelvedon, hauled by National Express liveried Class 90 No.90008. **James Welham**

90009 'Diamond Jubilee' (below) suitably adorned with the Union Jack on the body side is seen running into Colchester on 8th January 2014 with 1P33, the 11:30 Norwich - London Liverpool Street; note the re-liveried buffet car. Colchester station boasts the longest platform in the UK at 2,034ft long. **Nigel Gibbs**

…006 (top right) sports the rather striking 'One' livery, as it passes Lancaster's Crossing, Stowmarket, (circa. 2004) with a passenger express from Norwich to London Liverpool Street. The consist is a rake of Anglia aquamarine Mk2 vehicles. **Nick Slocombe**

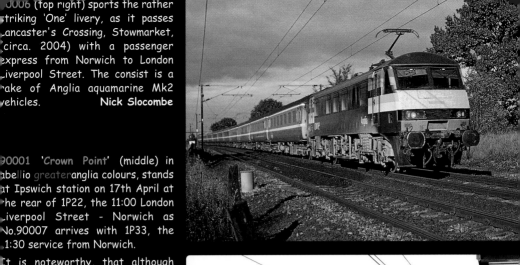

…0001 'Crown Point' (middle) in abellio greateranglia colours, stands at Ipswich station on 17th April at the rear of 1P22, the 11:00 London Liverpool Street - Norwich as No.90007 arrives with 1P33, the 1:30 service from Norwich.

It is noteworthy, that although there are only 50 Class 90s in the entire fleet, there have been more than 25 different liveries!

…0036 is the only loco to carry this variation of Railfreight Distribution livery, however it did not escape an EWS 'beasties' sticker!

On 23rd October 2007, No.90036 (below) waits to leave Ipswich with the 13:40hrs service from Norwich to London. **Martin Buck (2)**

90024 was repainted by EWS in GNER livery, without the GNER branding, supposedly to act as an ECML 'Thunderbird'. Here, No.90024 (above) sweeps into view at Old Linslade with 1M16, the 20:46 Inverness - London Euston Sleeper. (circa 2003).

Nick Slocombe

90029 (below) has arrived at the Border City of Carlisle on 24th March, standing at Citadel station's platform 4, with the first northbound sleeper; 1S25, the 21:16hrs service from London Euston, which conveys 'portions' for Fort William, Inverness and Aberdeen.

Keith McGovern

90024 (right), now adorned in 'Barbie' livery and allocated to Scotrail sleeper use, leaves Carstairs on 14th July 2011 with 1S26, the 23:50 London Euston - Glasgow Central. Both 'Up' and 'Down' sleeper services stop at Carstairs to attach/detach the Edinburgh Waverley portion.

Kenny Marrs

90029 (middle) is heading 1M16, 20:47 Inverness - London Euston sleeper on 15th July 2014, as it passes Acton Bridge, running slightly late. The reflection from the colour light signal glints off some of the vehicles in the lengthy consist.

Kenny Marrs

90024 (below), in First Scotrail livery, is resting in the confines of Wembley depot with Mk3 sleeper stock from one of the overnight Caledonian Sleeper services, which run six nights a week from London Euston to Scotland.

Once the stock has been serviced, the '90' and train will be hauled back into London Euston for another run to the north.

James Welham

Mail The aptly named No.90019 'Penny Black' (above) is in charge of 5M06, the 04:00 Glasgow Central - Euston empty TPO on 4th May 1993, which is seen passing Beck Foot **Neil Harvey (2**

90039 (below) tows failed Class 325 units Nos.325012, 325014 & 325016 past Castle Hill, south of Abington on 18th June 2014 forming 1M44, the 16:16 Shieldmuir - Warrington RMT. Although loco-hauled TPO/mail trains stopped running in January 2004, a handful of Class 325 operated mail trains were retained for Royal Mail use, albeit restricted to the WCML, running between Willesden - Warrington - Shieldmuir.

90016 (above) is stabled at London Euston station on 22nd October 1994 pending its next turn of duty. ReS (Rail Express Systems) came into existence in 1991 to handle mail trains across the network and their locos carried this livery of dark grey and red with blue markings.

This was at a time when ReS loco hauled mail trains operated out of the major London stations, prior to switching to a purpose built 'Railnet' terminal at Willesden, which opened in September 1996. This became the 'hub' of all mail train operations on the rail network.   **Ian Cuthbertson**

"This is the night mail, crossing the Border, bringing the cheque and postal order ....", the opening lines of W H Auden's famous poem, became synonymous with mail traffic.

90017 'Rail Express Systems' (below) sits at Crewe on 9th January 1997 with 1N93, the 20:06 Birmingham New Street - Preston Mail.   **Neil Harvey**

A faded looking No.90022 'Freightconnection' (above) speeds past Colton Junction on 10th August 1993 with an Edinburgh Waverley - Cambridge mail train, which comprises 12 vehicles; three blue & grey brake vans, a solitary blue 'GUV' and eight ReS/Royal Mail liveried vans.

Neil Harvey

90017 (above) streaks past All Saints, Offord Cluny's parish church, with 1A95, the 14:03 Low Fell - London King's Cross mail, formed of six vehicles.

Nick Slocomb

90039 (above) races along the North Sea Coast at Burnmouth on 30th March 2013, 'dragging' three 325 units (325012, 002, 016) on the diverted 1S80, Willesden - Shieldmuir mail. This working was diverted via the ECML on Easter Saturday due to engineering works on the WCML.

Steven Brynkilo

Some Class 90s were re-numbered into a "2" sub series after being fitted with modified brake blocks, to assist maintenance staff in making sure the right 'blocks' were fitted.

Carrying Railfreight Distribution International livery, No.90223 + No.90222 'Freightconnection' (above) stand at Preston, atop Class 325 EMU No.325008 'Peter Howarth CBE', which forms 5M89, the 11:32 Motherwell - Warrington RMT. This service was nominally booked for 2 x Class 325 units, although often worked by a single unit and, on occasions, used for stock transfers leading to this sight on 5th June 2000. Class 325 No.325004 is out of sight on the rear of the formation.

A shabby looking No.90239 (below) passes through Leyland on 19th December 2001 with an additional mail service from Shieldmuir to Bristol Parkway RMT, laid on to cater for the Christmas mail. **Fred Kerr (2)**

Class 90/2s

6X60

Innerwick : On 24th November 2014, DBS Class 90 No.90037 'Spirit of Dagenham' (above) passes Innerwick, near Torness nuclear power station, while working 6X60, the 12:35 Millerhill - Tyne Yard. This loco had only just returned to traffic after a long period in store at Crewe Electric.   **Steven Brykajlo**

Burnmouth : Looking out to sea on 5th December 2014, ScotRail liveried No.90019 (top right) is seen hugging the Berwickshire cliffs at Burnmouth and, as well as the usual empty rail carriers from the previous day's rail laying, 6X60 also includes some 'FEA' flats with empty green ballast boxes.   **Steven Brykajlo**

Monktonhall: DBS red No.90018 (opposite) has just crossed the River Esk after joining the ECML at Monktonhall Junction on 20th October 2014 with 6X60. The ECML originally crossed the River Esk to the right of the train but, with resignalling in the late '70s and the closure of the line to Smeaton and Dalkeith Pit, the ECML was realigned to cross the river using the bridge in this view.   **Keith McGovern**

Clifton : Having made its 'booked' stop in Morpeth Up Passenger Loop, 6X60 is seen passing Clifton (two miles south of Morpeth) on 21st October 2014 headed by No.90039 (below); Class 66/0 No.66187 is tucked inside 'DIT', hitching a ride to Tyne yard.   **Martin Cook**

Borders Railway

From October 2014, for a period of three months, the ECML is blessed with the rare sight of a Class 90 hauled freight service between Newcastle and Edinburgh, conveying rails for the new Border Railways being constructed to link Edinburgh Waverley and Tweedbank. The train service is:

6X90, 18:16 Tyne Yard - Millerhill   6X60, 12:35 Millerhill - Tyne Yard

The loco diagram utilises the Class 90 loco, which would otherwise sit all day at Edinburgh Waverley having worked the sleeper train to and from London Euston each night. The consist is five 'YEA' (Perch) Continuous Welded Rail Wagons:

DB 979084   DB 979089   DB 979133   DB 979077   DB 979090

The Borders Railway project involves constructing 30 miles of new line to Tweedbank on part of the former North British Railway 'Waverley' Route, which once ran for 98 miles linking Edinburgh and Carlisle.

The 'Waverley' opened in two stages between 1849 and 1865, closing in its entirety in January 1969.

On 13th May, the first test train runs over the new 'Borders Railway', DRS Class 37 No.37604 with DBSO 9702, working 1Q13, Millerhill - Tweedbank. Timetabled passenger services commence in September.

(Overleaf) :

Spittal : A truly sight. On 29th October 2014, Scotrail No.**90021** passes Spittal with 6X60 the 12:35 Millerhill Yard - Tyne Yard. The empty wagons are destined for Scunthorpe for reloading and another run back to Millerhill Yard where two GBRf 66s will top 'n' tail the train onto the Borders Railway.

Berwick-upon-Tweed is situated in the county of Northumberland, the northernmost town in England, lying at the mouth of the River Tweed, 2.5 miles south of the Scottish border. Also in view are the three bridges spanning the River Tweed which are, from front to back, the Berwick Bridge, Royal Tweed Bridge (A1167) and Royal Border Bridge. The latter, built between 1847 and 1850, was designed by Robert Stephenson (son of George Stephenson) for the York, Newcastle and Berwick Railway. It is 2,162 ft long, has 28 arches, each spanning 60 feet, 121 ft above the river.   **Martin Cook**

DBS replace Class 92s with Class 90s on all Anglo-Scottish intermodal and wagonload services from April, restricting the use of 92s to between Wembley and Dollands Moor.

On 10th June, Nos.90020 'Collingwood' + 90028 (above) are approaching Beattock Summit while working 4M25, the 06:06 Mossend - Daventry intermodal, both 90s in EWS Maroon & Gold livery.   **Steven Brykajlo**

(Previous Page) : **4M25 meets 6X65** .... not what was planned, but a great result all the same. Having been held in the loop at Abington, Nos.90035 + No.90024 head south with 4M25, Mossend - Daventry intermodal and meet No.90021 + No.90018 heading north with 6X65, Didcot - Mossend. The two pairs are seen about to pass each other on 7th August at Castle Hill, between Abington and Crawford.

DBS stickers are being applied to the Company's locos, as seen on No.90037 'Spirit of Dagenham' (below). It is double-headed with No.90020 'Collingwood' on 13th May, climbing Shap at Scout Green with 6S94, the 03:05 Dollands Moor - Irvine loaded china clay slurry tanks from Antwerp.   **Keith McGovern (2)**

6X65

90036 'Driver Jack Mills' + 90024 (right) pass through Carlisle Citadel station at 05:23hrs on 29th March with 6X65, 20:28 Didcot Yard - Mossend, consisting mainly of Ford vehicles from Dagenham.

Whilst other commodities, such as MoD stores, can be conveyed on this train service from Didcot, the main payload is invariably Ford vehicles, which reach Didcot Yard by means of a dedicated 6X44, 14:38hrs wagonload service from Dagenham. **Kenny Marrs**

'Driver Jack Mills'

Class 90 No.90036 'Driver Jack Mills' was named at Crewe in December 2014 to honour train driver Jack Mills (and second man, David Whitby) who took over the Glasgow Central - London Euston 'Up Postal' (1M44) at Crewe on the 8th August 1963, hauled by English Electric Class 40 No.D326 (later 40126).

The second carriage behind the loco was known as the 'HVP' (High Value Packages) coach, which carried large quantities of money and registered mail. Usually the value of the shipment would be around £300,000 but, due to a Bank Holiday weekend in Scotland, the total on the day was between £2.5 and £3 million.

Between Leighton Buzzard and Cheddington, the train was stopped at a tampered signal and resulted in £2.6 million being stolen and the assault on Jack Mills and David Whitby; both men never recovered from what happened, Jack Mills passed away in 1970, David Whitby, 2 years later.

Meanwhile, 6X65 wagonload service, hauled by the same pair of Class 90s (albeit with No.90024 leading), is seen again (above) on 3rd June in the beautiful Upper Clyde Valley, passing alongside the infant River Clyde at Wandel. The train is an impressive rake of loaded car carriers. **Steven Brykaile**

(Above) : This is the stretch of North Wales coast between Llandudno (visible to the right of the Great Orme on the left of the photo), and the city of Bangor. Specifically, this is between Penmeanmawr and Llanfairfechan.

Both the railway and the A55 North Wales Expressway have to hug the coast, to the point that there are two headlands that both pass through via tunnels. With government influence, millions has been spent on the road, while the railway has been left to almost fend for itself. Both go to the port at Holyhead, for access to the Republic of Ireland.

Some 30 / 40 years ago, Holyhead was a major container port, with daily freightliner services linking Birmingham (Lawley Street), London (Stratford / Willesden) and Manchester (Trafford Park). Today, those goods travel on the A55 and the freightliner terminal at Holyhead is now a car park.

On 9th June, DBS Class 67 No.67022 is seen at the rear of 1H89, the 13:01 Holyhead - Manchester Piccadilly, crossing the 13 arches of Pen-y-Clip viaduct, about to enter the western portal of Pen-y-Clip Avalanche Tunnel.

Of course, only from the sea can the magnificent engineering of the lower level railway viaduct and the elevated road (now eastbound only) be fully appreciated.   **Colin Partington**

ATW - Loco Hauled 2

From the start of the Winter timetable (Monday, 15th December 2014), an additional loco-hauled diagram comes into effect on the North Wales Coast, utilising a DBS Class 67 loco and some Mk3 coaches, procured from DB Regio and repainted at the Arriva LNWR works in Crewe.

This Arriva Trains Wales (ATW) is needed to release a Class 158 for the Cambrian lines around Machynlleth; the loco diagram is the former 'Northern Irishman' diagram that used to be worked by Class 57/3s a few years back.

Diagram   **Class 67 & DVT**

5D51, 06:55 Crewe CS - Crewe

1D51, 07:11 Crewe - Chester   1H82, 07:38 Chester - Manchester Piccadilly

5D34, 08:54 Manchester Picc.- Manchester Picc.*   1D34, 09:50 Manchester Picc. - Holyhead

1H89, 13:01 Holyhead - Manchester Picc.   5D31, 15:54 Manchester Picc.- Manchester Picc.*

1D31, 16:50 Manchester Picc. - Llandudno   1K96, 19:34 Llandudno - Crewe

5K96, 21:09 Crewe - Crewe CS

* (via Longsight Excursion Platform)

(Above) : 'Under the Wires' and a spot of 'bovver'. Station attendants at Warrington Bank Quay deal with a disruptive passenger on the ATW, 1D31 16:50 Manchester Piccadilly - Llandudno service, headed by Class 67 No.67001. Meantime, the driver looks on, probably wondering whether she'll be able to make up time.....the answer is no, as it happens. Already 17 minutes down on arrival at WBQ, a further seven minutes are lost dealing with the "incident", and eventual arrival in Llandudno will be 24 minutes late.

After WBQ, the train will leave the electrified section at Acton Grange Junction, crossing the Manchester Ship Canal, to follow the former London & North Western Railway route via Frodsham and Helsby to Chester, thence the North Wales Coast main line.   **David Hayes**

67001 in Chester

"Rear End Views" .... On 18th March, 1H89, the 13:01 Holyhead - Manchester Piccadilly is seen heading out of the City of Chester, making its way towards Helsby and Warrington, propelled by Class 67 No.67001 (above). The train has just passed the entrance (off Hoole Lane) to the old Chester shed (6A), which closed in 1967 and was demolished in 1973.

The A5268, St. Martin's Way, flyover straddles the western approach to Chester, prior to the main line going through Northgate Street and Windmill Lane Tunnel. Here, on 28th January, No.67001 (below) is seen propelling 1H89 under the flyover, just under a mile from the station.

1K96 : The vapour trails suggest there's been a fair bit of aircraft activity in the sky above Chester station on 20th May, as Arriva Trains Wales Class 67 No.67001 (above) awaits departure time at the rear of 1K96, the 19:34 Llandudno - Crewe.

Same day, same train but this time an interesting composition of No.67001 (below) viewed through the lattice framework of the station footbridge. Chester station acts as a meeting point for lines coming in from Crewe, Wrexham, Holyhead, Hooton, Warrington and Altrincham. **Colin Partington (4)**

FRODSHAM

Weaver Navigation : On 15th May, No.67001 (above) is seen from the A56, which links Frodsham and Sutton Weaver, crossing Weston Viaduct (Weaver Navigation) with 1D34, the 09:50 Manchester Piccadilly - Holyhead service. Beyond, is the M56 Motorway.

The author fondly remembers **1D34** in the early '80s, one leg of the well known 'Bangor' diagram between Manchester Victoria and Bangor; a good candidate for a Class 40 and 400 miles of the best English Electric could offer! Once on the diagram, the same loco could stay on it for several weeks!   **Colin Partington**

River Weaver : No.67001 (below) crosses the River Weaver on 9th April with 1D34, the 09:50 Manchester Piccadilly - Holyhead. The barge is MV'Progress', a chemical/oil tanker built in 1965, formerly named 'Henty Progress', 'Deepdale H' and 'Riverbeacon'.   **Neil Harvey**

'ENGLISH ELECTRIC RETRO'

The new North Wales Coast loco-hauled diagram, linking Crewe / Manchester with Holyhead / Llandudno, brings back fond memories of my time spent on 'the coast' chasing and photographing locos, especially Class 40s in the early 1980s.

COLWYN BAY : Looking out across the Bay towards the Victoria Pier, No.**37414** 'Cathays C & W Works 1846-1993' (above) passes over the A55 road at Old Conwy on 2nd May 1997 with 1K65, the 12:22 Bangor - Crewe. The loco is on a gradient of 1 in 100 at this point, climbing above the Old Colwyn Sea Wall defences, about to enter Penmaenrhos Tunnel.

The entire train set is formed of matching Regional Railways colours and, at this time, Class 37/4 + Mk1/Mk2s train sets formed the basis of passenger services linking Birmingham International / Crewe and Bangor / Holyhead. They proved to be very popular with rail enthusiasts. **Martin Buck**

LLANDUDNO JUNCTION : At a time when semaphore signals controlled the area around Llandudno Junction, Class 40 No.**40035** (above) slows for the Llandudno Junction station stop with 1A56, the 13:00 Holyhead - London Euston 'boat train' on 25th July 1980. This particular service ran non-stop from here to Chester and was often hauled by a pair of Class 40s - wonderful!

HOLYHEAD : Centre panel headcode Class 40 No.**40194** (below) waits for the station pilot (08) to release the stock off 1J53, the 1D29, the 10:45 Manchester Victoria - Holyhead, so it can work the 15:17 hrs departure back to Manchester. MV 'St. Columba' prepares for the next sailing to Dun Laoghaire.

CHESTER : The last Class 40 to remain in BR Green livery was No.**40106** (above), which is seen entering Chester on 7th June 1980 with an unidentified express. Note the milepost, denoting 179 miles from London Euston. No.40106 was withdrawn from BR operating stock on 17th April 1983 and fortunately preserved on the Great Central Railway, now named 'Atlantic Conveyor'.

  COLWYN BAY : No.**40115** (below), a loco which had its underslung water tanks removed when its steam heating boiler was isolated, enters Colwyn Bay station on 1J30, the 11:30 Bangor - Manchester Victoria. This service was the second leg of the 'Bangor' diagram.   **Martin Buck (4)**

'Prepping' the 92s

(Above) : On 24th March there is the unusual sight of a Class 92 + Class 66/7 combination working a coal train on the ECML. Actually, this is a trial outing for GBRf Class 92 No.92033, prior to taking up new sleeper duties on the WCML from 1st April. No 92033 + No.66749 pass Joan Croft Junction with 4S45, the 11:28 Doncaster Down Decoy – Hunterston, the 92 only going as far as Tyne Yard. **Pauline McKenna**

(Below) : A second Class 92 decked out in Caledonian Sleeper colours is No.92018, which is seen on 17th March out on trial. It is double headed with GBRf Class 66/7 No.66709 'Sorrento' passing through Runcorn station with 6L48, the 15:49 Garston - Dagenham car carriers; the 92 coming off at Crewe. Also in view is the Runcorn (Silver Jubilee) Bridge, which crosses the River Mersey and the Manchester Ship Canal at Runcorn Gap between Runcorn and Widnes. Its main arch span is 1,082 feet and the bridge opened in 1961 as a replacement for the Widnes-Runcorn Transporter Bridge. **Fred Kerr**

Background

The **Caledonian Sleeper** is a an overnight, Anglo-Scottish, sleeper train service, which connects London Euston with Aberdeen, Edinburgh, Fort William, Glasgow and Inverness.

From 1st April, **Serco Caledonian Sleepers Limited**, a subsidiary of Serco, now operate the Caledonian Sleeper as an independent franchise, split from the ScotRail franchise, formerly operated by FirstGroup.

GBRf replace DBS as traction provider on the WCML, booked for Class 92 operation, but operational problems with the Class 92s persist throughout the year; in August, Freightliner Class 90s are hired in as cover for the errant Class 92s.

The Train Services (northbound shown)

Highland Sleeper : **1S25, 21:16 London Euston - Inverness**

The train calls at Watford Junction, Crewe and Preston to pick up passengers only, and arrives at Edinburgh Waverley approximately six-and-a-half hours later. At Edinburgh, the electric loco is uncoupled and replaced by three Class 67s, one for each of the three portions, viz:

1S25, 21:16 Edinburgh Waverley - Inverness	Class 67
1Y11, 04:50 Edinburgh Waverley - Fort William	Class 67
1A25, 04:40 Edinburgh Waverley - Aberdeen	Class 67

The front three coaches of the combined train go to Fort William, the middle portion for Aberdeen and the rear portion for Inverness.

Lowland Sleeper : **1S26, 23:50   London Euston - Glasgow Central**

The train picks up passengers at Watford Junction only and passengers can alight at Carlisle and at Carstairs, where the train divides, the rear portion continuing to Edinburgh, running as:

1B26, 06:34 Carstairs - Edinburgh Waverley   Class 92

(Above) : Running 50 minutes late, GBRf Class 92 No.92032 'IMech E Railway Division' (above) passes through Prestonpans at 00:22hrs on 8th June with 1M11, the diverted 23:40 Glasgow Central - London Euston sleeper. What makes this image noteworthy, is that No.92032 is travelling in excess of 60mph, captured using camera settings of ISO 25600 and a shutter speed of 1/320 at f4.5!   **Keith McGovern**

(Left) : Class 92 No.**92033** is looking resplendent in new Caledonian Sleeper colours, waiting to leave Glasgow Central on 1st April with the first southbound train to run under the new regime.

The train is 1M11, the 23:40 Glasgow Central - London Euston.

(Middle) : After the failure of a GBRf Class 92 due to faulty ETH, No.**87002** '**Royal Sovereign**' is duly commandeered to work 1S25, the 21:16 London Euston - Inverness from Wembley Yard.

It is seen here resting at Edinburgh Waverley on 15th April before returning with 1M16 back to London Euston.　　　　**Guy Houston (2)**

(Below) : Here's No.**87002** out working again, this time on the morning of 28th April, passing Harrow & Wealdstone with the 16 coaches which form 1M16, the 20:44 Inverness - London Euston.

Nigel Gibbs

126

Deep in Great Northern territory GBRf 'Dyson' No.92033 (above) passes Harringay on the 'Up Fast' line with the diverted Serco 'Caledonian sleeper' - 1M16, 20:25 Inverness - London Euston.　　　**Nigel Gibbs**

No.87002 'Royal Sovereign' (below) is seen again, on 15th April standing at Platform 6, Crewe, during its booked three minute stop with 1S25, the 21:16 London Euston - Inverness sleeper.　　　**Mick Tindall**

What starts off so well on 14th April, did not end well for Class 92 No.92028 'Saint Saens' (above) which was the booked loco for 1M11, the 23:40 Glasgow Central - London Euston sleeper service.

The GBRF 'Euorporte' branded loco sits atop 1M11 at Glasgow Central, prior to departure. Unfortunately, it does not complete the full 401 mile journey to the English Capital, having been declared a failure at Milton Keynes ....

.... Class 92 No.92032 'IMech E Railway Division' (below) is now seen heading 1M11 the next morning, passing Ledburn. It is assisting No.92028 'Saint Saens' on the ECS off 1M11, the 23:40 Glasgow Central - London Euston that had terminated at Milton Keynes after the failure of No.92028; the train is now en route to Wembley depot.   **Guy Houston / Nigel Gibbs**

WCML Sleeper Diagrams (Electric Hauled Legs)

Electric 1
5M11, 21:07 Polmadie CMD - Glasgow Central   (Loco on rear)
1M11, 23:40 Glasgow Central - London Euston
5M11, 08:27 London Euston - Wembley Intercity Depot   (Loco on rear)

Electric 2
5S26, 21:40 Wembley Intercity Depot - London Euston   (Loco on rear)
1S26, 23:50 London Euston - Glasgow Central
5S26, 08:09 Glasgow Central - Polmadie CMD   (Loco on rear)

Electric 3
5S95, 19:34 Wembley Intercity Depot - London Euston   (Loco on rear)
1S25, 21:16 London Euston - Inverness   (To Edinburgh)

Electric 4
5C11, 20:43 Polmadie CMD - Edinburgh Waverley
1M16, 01:38 Edinburgh Waverley - London Euston
5M16, 09:27 London Euston - Wembley Intercity Depot

Electric 5   (Diagram can be worked by 47 / 67)
5C11, 20:43 Polmadie CMD - Edinburgh Waverley
1C11, 23:40 Edinburgh Waverley - Carstairs
1B26, 06:34 Carstairs - Edinburgh Waverley
5B26, 08:18 Edinburgh Waverley - Polmadie CMD

Electric 6   (Diagram covered by any spare loco)
5M11, 21:07 Polmadie - Glasgow Central
5S26, 08:09 Glasgow Central - Polmadie CMD

ACLG 1
0M11, 06:55 Wembley EFOC - London Euston   (Light Engine)
5M11, 08:27 London Euston - Wembley Intercity Depot
5S96, 21:40 Wembley Intercity Depot - London Euston
0A96, 23:53 London Euston - Wembley EFOC   (Light Engine)

ACLG 2
5M16, 09:27 London Euston - Wembley Intercity Depot
5S95, 19:34 Wembley Intercity Depot - London Euston

Selective Images :

(Inset) : This is the new logo for the Caledonian Sleeper, one which is already synonymous with the 'Fort Bill' - London route, known as the 'Deerstalker' to many. The 'White Stag' is more contemporary with the five point antlers representing the three Highland and two Lowland destinations.   **Simon Howard**

(Overleaf) 'Night & Day'

On 22nd July, under the impressive roof of Glasgow Central, several trains await their late-night departures including GBRf Class 92 No.92038 (Page 130), which is at the head of 1M11, the 23:40 Glasgow Central - London Euston. The others are (from left to right) No.380110 on 1G05, the 22:50hrs to Gourock, No.380101 on 1K69 and No.380114 on 1K71, the 22:30hrs and 23:00hrs services to Ayr, respectively.   **Chris Williams**

(Overleaf) : 87002 'Royal Sovereign' (Page 131) gets more exercise than just hauling the ECS between Wembley and Euston, working the 'Highland Sleeper' between London Euston and Edinburgh Waverley. This is 1M16, the 20:25 Inverness - London Euston on 18th April, running slightly ahead of schedule at Hademore, near Lichfield, just catching the first rays of the sun.   **John Whitehouse**

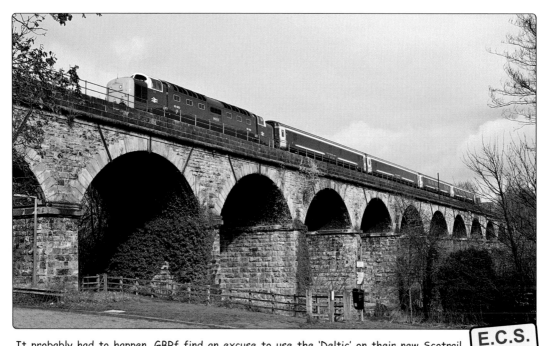

E.C.S.

It probably had to happen, GBRf find an excuse to use the 'Deltic' on their new Scotrail sleeper contract. Here, a move of stock for maintenance is the order of the day (5Z55, Inverness - Polmadie) using the 'Deltic', which would otherwise be spare in Glasgow works for EMU stock moves to / from Shields depot. No.**55003 'Meld'** (above), a disguised No.55022 'Royal Scots Grey', crosses Larbert Viaduct on 27th March. The coaching stock is Nos.10693, 10580, 9802 and 6701.

GBRf move a pair of Class 47s north to help with ECS and diversions. 'Heritage' Large Logo Class 47/4 No.**47847** (below) makes a visit to Glasgow Central on 24th April with 5M11 ECS from Polmadie. The train has been moved onto Platform 9 as the usual Platform 10 is occupied by a Class 380 unit, apparently parked up for the night! Photography at this Scottish terminus can be problematic, as station staff often crack down on the use of tripods in the interest of health & safety! **Guy Houston (2)**

Class 47/4 No.**47812** (above) is seen on 23rd May with the diverted Caledonian Sleeper ECS off 1B26 from Edinburgh (5B26, 08:18 Edinburgh Waverley - Polmadie CMD), passing Hartwood on the Kirknewton - Shotts - Holytown line. Due to engineering work, the 'booked' route via Carstairs is closed. The loco which worked into Edinburgh, No.**92044**, is on the rear. **Alastair Blackwood**

Class 86/1 No.**86101** **'Sir William A Stanier FRS'** (below) passes Willesden depot on 4th April, heading back to Wembley with 5M11 ECS off 1M11, the 23:40 Glasgow Central - London Euston overnight sleeper. This loco will see use entirely on ECS moves in and out of Euston and is on hire to GBRf from the AC Locomotive Group, along with No.**86401** and Class 87 No.**87002** 'Royal Sovereign'. **Simon Howard**

Extra Capacity

18th May : a new timetable sees the introduction of two loco-hauled trains to add much needed extra seating, working the Cumbrian Coast between Preston - Barrow in Furness - Carlisle.

The deal, brokered by Northern Rail and the Department of Transport, is to release rolling stock to strengthen other services. Two Class 156 sets go to Trans Pennine to offset a loss of some Class 170s.

MILLOM : The driver piles on the power as No.37609 (above) roars away from Millom with 2C41, the 14:37 Barrow in Furness - Carlisle. St. George's Church stands proud in the background, its steeple being the biggest landmark in the town.   **Neil Harvey**

Additional loco-hauled trains on the Cumbrian Coast are not uncommon; in November 2009 a temporary timetable was introduced following the closure of the line in Workington as a result of heavy rainfall.

Two diagrams are involved featuring DRS Class 37s in top 'n' tail formation. DBSOs arrive late July to displace one Class 37 on each diagram, but here's the initial workings:

Diagram 1	Class 37 + 3 Mk2e + Mk2f + Class 37		Weekdays	
2C32, 05:15 Carlisle - Preston			2C47, 10:04 Preston - Barrow in Furness	
5C47, 11:42 Barrow in Furness - Barrow CS			5C41, 14:25 Barrow CS - Barrow in Furness	
2C41, 14:37 Barrow in Furness - Carlisle			2C42, 17:37 Carlisle - Barrow in Furness	
5C42, 20:38 Barrow in Furness - Barrow CS				

Diagram 2	Class 37 + 3 Mk2e + Mk2f + Class 37		Weekdays	
2C33, 05:46 Barrow in Furness - Carlisle			2C40, 08:42 Carlisle - Barrow in Furness	
2C49, 11:38 Barrow in Furness - Carlisle			2C34, 14:35 Carlisle - Barrow in Furness	
2C47, 17:31 Barrow in Furness - Carlisle			5C47, 20:41 Carlisle - Carlisle Kingmoor DRS	

CARLISLE CITADEL : As one journey ends, another begins ......

No.37419 'Carl Havilland' (left) waits to leave on 15th June with 2C42, the 17:37hrs service to Barrow-in-Furness, having been on the rear of 2C41 from Barrow.

There are actually three 37s here, gently idling away the time; No.37419, plus No.37423 on the rear of 2C42 (out of sight) and No.37609 stabled behind No.57012.

Colin Partington

LANCASTER : DRS Class 37/4 No.**37423** **'Spirit Of The Lakes'** (above) explodes into action leaving Lancaster on 20th June with 2C31, the 17:31 Lancaster - Barrow in Furness.

A touch of irony? The photographer wishes to study 'Earth & Environmental Sciences' at Lancaster University, but his two main interests (Earth & the Environment and 'claggy' English Electric locos) would seem to contradict one another!

PRESTON : Having just brought in 2C32 from Carlisle, No.**37401** **'Mary Queen of Scots'** (below) stands at Preston on 30th July waiting to trail 2C47, the 10:04hrs service back to Barrow-in-Furness. No.37603 now becomes the main train engine.

Chris Williams (2)

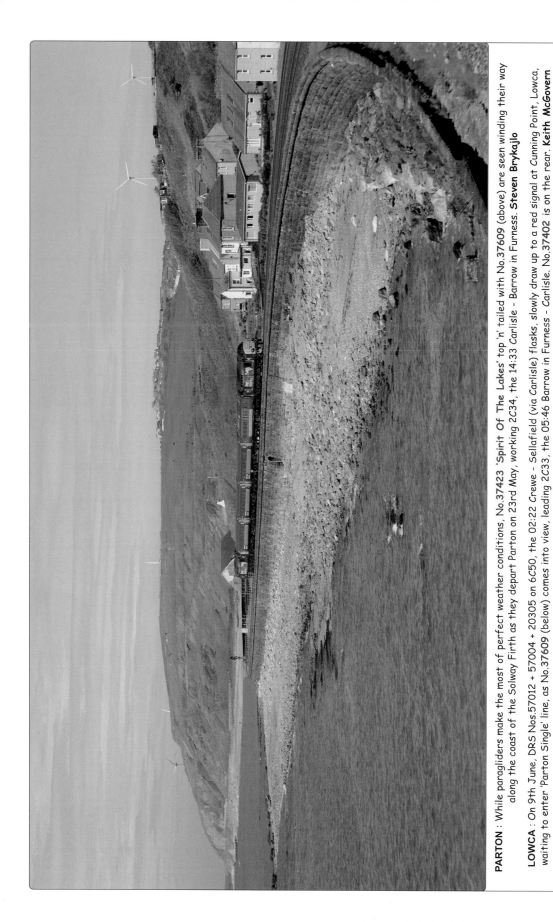

PARTON : While paragliders make the most of perfect weather conditions, No.37423 'Spirit Of The Lakes' top 'n' tailed with No.37609 (above) are seen winding their way along the coast of the Solway Firth as they depart Parton on 23rd May, working 2C34, the 14:33 Carlisle - Barrow in Furness. **Steven Brykajlo**

LOWCA : On 9th June, DRS Nos.57012 + 57004 + 20305 on 6C50, the 02:22 Crewe - Sellafield (via Carlisle) flasks, slowly draw up to a red signal at Cunning Point, Lowca, waiting to enter 'Parton Single' line, as No.37609 (below) comes into view, leading 2C33, the 05:46 Barrow in Furness - Carlisle. No.37402 is on the rear. **Keith McGovern**

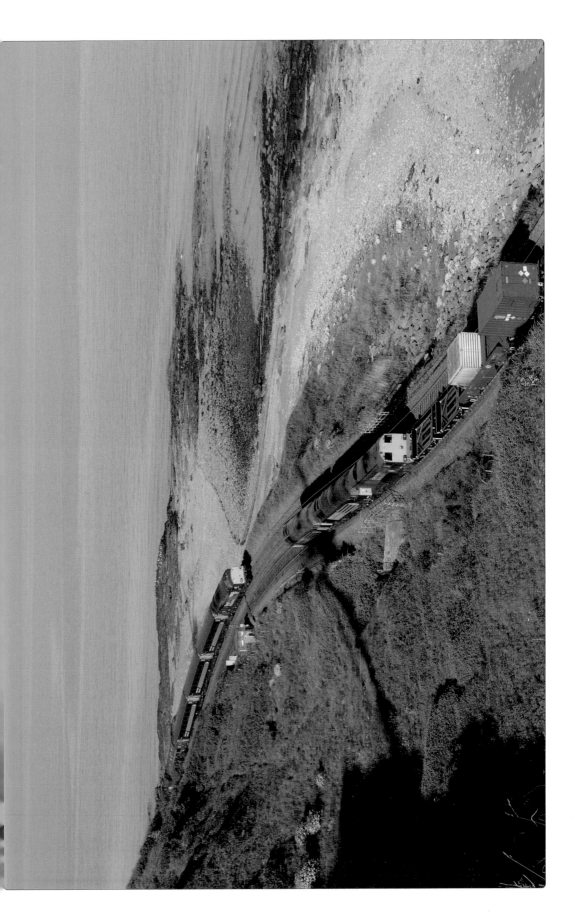

DUNNERHOLME : No.37423 'Spirit Of The Lakes' top 'n' tailed with No.37609 (above) pass Dunnerholme on 20th May with 2C34, the 14:35 Carlisle - Barrow in Furness. Dunnerholme is between Kirkby-in-Furness and Askam in Furness on the shores of the Duddon Estuary.

GREEN ROAD : On 3rd June, No.37688 'Kingmoor TMD' (below) approaches Green Road station with 2C49, the 11:38 Barrow in Furness - Carlisle; No.37423 'Spirit Of The Lakes' is on the rear. There really can be few locations in the UK with a better backdrop than the Cumbrian Fells.   **Neil Harvey (2)**

Kent Viaduct

On 11th July, No.37603 and No.37423 'Spirit Of The Lakes' (above) cross Kent Viaduct (552 yards long with 50 piers, built in 1857) at Arnside with 2C47, the 10:04 Preston - Barrow in Furness. This composition shows off the scale and beauty of the area and the Lake District beyond - stunning!   **Chris Williams**

Eskmeals Viaduct

Meanwhile, on the viaduct the same day, No.37419 'Carl Havilland' leads No.37423 'Spirit Of The Lakes' (below), heads 2C34, the 14:35 Carlisle - Barrow in Furness. The 18 span, 330 yards long, viaduct crosses the River Esk, built originally for the Whitehaven & Furness Junction Railway.   **Neil Harvey**

FOXFIELD : Having crossed the estuary via Duddon Viaduct (visible in the background), No.37401 'Mary Queen of Scots' (above) accelerates away from Foxfield at Angerton on 9th August with 2C32, the 05:15 Carlisle – Barrow In Furness; No.37402 tails. **Ian Ball**

PARTON : *On the Sea Wall* .... DRS Class 37/5 No.37688 'Kingmoor TMD' + No.37423 'Spirit Of The Lakes' (below) top 'n' tail 2C47, the 17:31 Barrow in Furness - Carlisle on 3rd June, approaching Parton station. A fellow photographer has positioned himself nearer to the sea wall for his own take on proceedings. **Neil Harvey**

Test Train Debut

Network Rail opt for Colas Class 37s to replace their Class 31s on measurement trains and, on 5th July, Nos.37175 and 37219 top 'n' tail PLPR1, to work between Retford - Doncaster and York - Malton.

The 37s are out again on 6th and 7th July visiting the 'Grimsby Light Railway' system and Drax power station branch, respectively. Here are the details:

7th July : 1Q07, 11:50 Doncaster West Yard - Derby RTC

Location	Pass	Arrive	Depart
DONCASTER WEST YARD			**11:50**
Shaftholme Junction	11:55		
Knottingley East Junction	12:14		
Whitley Bridge Junction	12:26		
Drax Power station	12:52		
Whitley Bridge Junction	13:11		
Knottingley	**13:24**		
Pontefract Monkhill	**13:31**		
Castleford	**13:41**		
Church Fenton		**14:10**	**14:32**
Gascoigne Wood Junction	14:43		
Selby	**14:53**		
Barlby Loops		14;55	15:59
Selby	**16:01**		
Gascoigne Wood Junction	16:13		
Church Fenton		**16:19**	**16:29**
Castleford		**17:01**	**17:13**
Normanton	**17:21**		
Calder Bridge Junction	17:28		
Hare Park Junction	17:36		
Fitzwilliam	**17:39**		
South Kirkby Junction	17:42		
Moorthorpe	**17:44**		
Swinton	**17:56**		
Masborough Junction	18:01		
Meadowhall	**18:03**		
Sheffield Midland	**18:16**		
Heeley Up Loop		18:24	18:35
Chesterfield		**18:52**	**19:12**
Chesterfield South Junction		19:14	19:19
Ambergate Junction	19:33		
Derby	**19:43**		
DERBY RTC	**19:46**		

(Selective Images) :

(top right) : Colas Class 37/0s, No.37175 (front) and No.37219 (rear), pass Hagg Lane, Gascoigne Wood, on 7th July working 1Q07, the 11:50 Doncaster West Yard - Derby RTC in top 'n' tail mode; this being the Barlby Loop to Church Fenton leg of the 'trip'.

(bottom right) : No.37219 leads through Warmfield, Goose Hill, with 1Q07, as the sun pops out to shine on the colourful formation! Goose Hill was the junction where the former Midland Route deviated via Cudworth - Grimethorpe - Wath Road Junction, but closed in the 1980s due to mining subsidence.   **Neil Harvey (2)**

On 6th July, Colas Class 37/0s, No.37175 and No.37219 are out working 1Q06, the 09:42 Doncaster West Yard - Doncaster West Yard, testing some North East Lincolnshire branch lines, including Barton Upon Humber and Cleethorpes.

(above) : No.37175 leads the returning 1Q06 through Thornton Abbey on the Barton on Humber branch - photographs of loco hauled trains on this line are rare, to say the least!

(opposite) : Earlier on the outward leg, No.37175 ambles along the 'Up Slow' line at Barnetby making its way to Humber Road Junction, where the train will reverse and head for the Barton on Humber branch.

(below) : Back on the Barton branch, No.37219 leads 1Q06 into Goxhill station and past the signal box controlling the level crossing, which still retains traditional crossing gates on big concrete posts. Not many timbered gates survive these days, many having been replaced with lifting barriers.   **Duncan Scott (3)**

1Q06

6th July : 1Q06, 09:42 Doncaster West Yard - Doncaster West Yard

Location	Pass	Arrive	Depart
DONCASTER WEST YARD			**09:42**
Bentley Junction	09:44		
Hatfield & Stainforth	**09:49**		
Scunthorpe	**10:07**		
Scunthorpe West Junction	10:08		
Wrawby Junction	10:26		
Barnetby	**10:29**		
Marsh West Junction	10:50		
Immingham East Junction	11:21		
Humber Road Junction		11:35	11:43
Great Coates No1 Junction	12:13		
Marsh West Junction	12:16		
Habrough Junction	12:26		
Ulceby	12:27		
Barton-on-Humber		**12:52**	**13:02**
Thornton Abbey		13:21	13;56
Habrough Junction	14:01		
Cleethorpes		**14:18**	**15:08**
Grimsby Docks		15:13	15:14
Grimsby Town		15:16	15:17
Barnetby		**15;39**	
Wrawby Junction		15:41	16:01
Barnetby	**16:03**		
Barnetby Signal Be27		16:07	16:15
Barnetby		**16:19**	
Wrawby Junction	16:21		
Scunthorpe West Junction		16:42	17:12
Scunthorpe	**17:14**		
Hatfield & Stainforth	**17:31**		
Bentley Junction	17:37		
Doncaster West Yard	**17:42**		

Class 37 No.37175 + No.37219 (above) pass through Selby station with 1Q07 test train, having traversed Selby Swing Bridge. The swing bridge was built for the North Eastern Railway and carries the railway line from Leeds to Hull over the River Ouse; once part of the original ECML.　　Pauline McKenna

Nos. **50017 'Royal Oak** + **50007 'Hercules'** (above) head 6Z08, the 10:22 Boston Docks - Washwood Heath loaded steel through Burton-on-Trent, in a welcome patch of sunshine. The use of a **'Zulu'** headcode instead of the usual 6M08, reflects the use of 'non-standard' locos on this particular service!

Mick Tindall

50017 'Royal Oak'

It seems Colas Rail have developed a certain penchant for Class 50s, especially allowing 'new to the main line' locos to be tested on scheduled freight services, like the Boston Docks steel (6M08 / 6E07) service.

Just like in 2014, when No.50007 'Hercules' was 'trialled' on this service, No.50017 'Royal Oak' returns to main line running on the same flow on 19th May.

(Top / inset) : Here it comes! No.**50017 'Royal Oak'**, double-headed with No.50007 'Hercules'. has been given a clear path through Elford with 6Z08, the 10:22 Boston Docks - Washwood Heath loaded steel, in preference to 6M57, the 07:15 Lindsey - Kingsbury, waiting in the loop, hauled by Class 60 No.60054. By the time the 50s reach Elford, the weather takes a turn for the worse. **Craig Adamson (2)**

Key Facts

Built	BREL, Crewe	
In Traffic	April 1968	
Allocations	From new	: Crewe Diesel Depot
	May 1974	: Plymouth, Laira TMD.
Numbers	From new	: D417
	February 1974	: 50017'
Name	April 1978	: 'Royal Oak'
Livery	From New	: BR Blue
	December 1983	: BR Blue, Large Logo
	June 1986	: Network South East
Withdrawn	September 1991	
Present Time	Preserved : Boden Rail Engineering	

Notes

(1) As D417, this was the only Class 50 to use its weight transfer equipment.

(2) 50017 was briefly transferred back to the Midland Region, until January 1976.

(3) 'Royal Oak' name formerly carried by Class 43 NBL 'Warship' No.D842.

(4) No.50017 named after the Royal Navy Revenge-class battleship 'Royal Oak'....

HMS 'Royal Oak' built during the First World War; launched 1914 and completed in 1916.

HMS 'Royal Oak' first saw combat at the Battle of Jutland as part of the Grand Fleet.

HMS 'Royal Oak' torpedoed on 14th October 1939 by German submarine U-47, while anchored at Scapa Flow in Orkney, Scotland.

BREL Doncaster took over the refurbishment of the Class 50 fleet from Crewe. By late 1978, *'The Plant'* was ready to receive its first locos; the first two being No.50006 'Neptune' and No.50017 'Royal Oak'.

In original blue livery, No.**50017 'Royal Oak'** (above) is seen waiting outside the works and, after refurbishment, No.50017 became one of only six Class 50s (001, 006, 013, 017, 019 and 047) to be refurbished without the application of Large Logo double arrows on the body side. Note the blanking plate on the front end in readiness for a headlight to be fitted. **Martin Buck**

Assorted Liveries **NETWORK SOUTH EAST** : This livery was launched in June 1986, although No.**50017** 'Royal Oak' (above) carries a later version. The loco approaches Radley on 30th June 1988 with 1F52, the 17:32 London Paddington - Oxford which, amazingly, from Reading was an 'all stations' service, so passengers at Radley would have 11 coaches to choose from, rather than the equivalent three of today. Note the former point work for the Abingdon branch, which closed in 1984. Although the majority of the track was lifted shortly afterwards, the two points visible here survived a little longer.

RAILFREIGHT TWO TONE GREY : No.50017 'Royal Oak', running as No.**50117** (above), + No.50015 'Valiant', catch the last rays of the setting sun as they accelerate away from Blue Anchor with the 17:25hrs Bishops Lydeard - Minehead service on 19th September 1998. During the West Somerset Railway's Diesel Gala, No.50017 ran as No.50117 and in Railfreight General livery, had the loco followed the example of No.50049 and been converted for purely freight use.

BR BLUE, LARGE LOGO : From August 1980, Class 50s started to receive BR Blue Large Logo livery. With the outskirts of Cardiff visible in the background, Large Logo No.50017 'Royal Oak' (above) passes Marshfield on 28th April 1984 with the 1O67 08:05 Cardiff Central to Portsmouth Harbour. There seems to be plenty of first class accommodation on this train, with nearly half the train probably empty as a result!

LMS GOLD STRIPE MAROON : Surely the strangest livery ever to adorn a Class 50. No 50017 (below) passes Bredicot on 24 June 2000 in the company of No.**47703** with a northbound VSOE 'Northern Belle; very Art Deco, with gold banding and numbers. Although totally unauthentic, it looked quite good when clean, as here. However, it's use on the mainline in this condition was short lived.   **Martin Loader (4)**

151

On The Logs 60002 becomes the first Colas Class 60 on 21st April to work a timber train over the Settle & Carlisle, when it pilots No.66849 'Wylam Dilly' on 6J37, 12:58 Carlisle Yard - Chirk. No.60002 + No.66849 (above) are passing Salt Lake Cottages on the Settle & Carlisle, running to the 'Up Goods Loop' at Hellifield where the 'tug' will come off. No.66849, ever-present on the 'logs' at the time, will then proceed on its own for the remainder of the journey.

At Hellifield, No.60002 (below) is seen framed by semaphore signals and one of the ornate LMS stanchions which support the station canopy. The 'tug' is running onto the 'Up Shipley' main line, where it will reverse onto the 'Down Main' line for the return to Carlisle. **Neil Harvey (2)**

60002

Background

Of the Class 60s secured by Colas Rail from DBS in 2014, No.60002 becomes the first one to re-enter traffic in 2015; the fifth in total, following Nos.60021, 60076, 60085 and 60087.

History

In Traffic	: December 1992		
First Depot Allocation	: Immingham		
Final Depot Allocation	: Toton		
Owners	: December 1992	: British Rail	
	April 1996	: EWS	
	November 2007	: DBS	
	March 2014	: Colas Rail	
Withdrawn	: December 2008		
Reinstated (Colas)	: December 2014		
Names	: December 1992	: Capability Brown	
	: February 1998	: High Peak	

No.60002 (above) shows off Colas colours to good effect, as it passes Lostock Hall Junction on 25th March with 6E32, the 08:40 Preston Docks - Lindsey. Meanwhile, a 2-Car 'Pacer' DMU can be seen leaving Lostock Hall with 2S17, the 08:23 Colne - Blackpool South; the line to the left leads to Farington Junction / WCML.   **Fred Kerr**

(Overleaf) : Having excitedly headed up to Todmorden on 25th March, with a promise of "cloudless blue skies", the photographer arrives to find clouds and several that decide to remain persistently over the Copy Pit and Portsmouth area. However, the outcome is still rewarding, No.60002 (Page 154) descends from Copy Pit with 6E32, Preston Docks - Lindsey discharged bitumen tanks. The hamlet in the foreground is the Yorkshire village of Portsmouth and the train is currently in Lancashire!   **David Hayes**

Meanwhile, four months later, No.60002 (Page 155) is seen approaching Patchway with 6M18, the 06:58 Margam TC - Washwood Heath loaded steel carriers, running along the lower 'Up' line, having emerged from the south portal of Patchway New Tunnel; note the purple Rosebay Willowherb.   **Mark Pike**

Retro 002

TWO TONE GREY : A little reminiscing from the archives, captures a freight flow which has long since ceased. No.60002 'Capability Brown' (above) passes Melton Ross, near Barnetby, on 1st October 1996 with empty red gypsum waste containers, which formed 6D86, the 12:50 Roxby - Grimsby. The waste originated from the Tioxide UK plant in Grimsby.   **Peter Slater**

EWS MAROON & GOLD : **"High Peak in the High Peak"** .... No.60002 'High Peak' (below) is seen at New Mills South Junction on 4th October 2002 with 6H43, the 08:50 Pendleton - Tunstead limestone empties, formed of Buxton Lime Industries branded 'JGA' bogie hoppers.

The signal box is a Midland Railway type 3b design, which opened in June 1903 in connection with the quadrupling of the line to Bugsworth Junction. It was refurbished by Network Rail in the early 2000s with uPVC cladding and windows.   **Neil Harvey**

"ON TEST"

No.**60002 'Capability Brown'** (right) is at the Brush Works, Loughborough, where it is undergoing tests prior to its release into traffic. The livery is two tone grey, complete with petroleum sector decals of blue and yellow waves.

Ian Cuthbertson

HOME BASE

Home for all Class 60s was Toton, but 'out-based' at depots around the network, including Cardiff, Immingham, Thornaby, Stewarts Lane and Wigan Springs Branch.

Inside Immingham TMD on 7th August 2006, No.60002 (below), now named **'High Peak'**, is sandwiched between team mates No.60090 'Quinag' and No.60010.

Loco servicing at Immingham ceased in April 2009.

A steam shed was originally built here by the Great Central Railway in 1912 to service the new Immingham Docks.

Craig Adamson (2)

'Before & After'

Class 66/7 No.66711 (left), in original 'Bluebird' livery, leaves Ferme Park on 28th June 2012, travelling along the GN 'Down Slow No.2' line, past Harringay with 6M09, 11:40 Ferme Park - Wellingborough departmental.

The train is about to go onto the Tottenham & Hampstead Line, heading for the Midland Main Line via Carlton Road Junction. **Nigel Gibbs**

No.66711 (middle) is passing through Paddock Wood station on 16th May, with 6G10, Faversham - Hoo Junction return engineer's 'trip'. Look closely and you should be able to identify 10 different types of departmental wagon in the consist. **Alan Hazelden**

No.66711 (below) is passing Quainton Road on 21st May with a rake of 'JNAs' full of spoil, running as 6M92, the 12.32 Willesden ET - Calvert.

This delightful station opened in 1868, built by the Aylesbury and Buckingham Railway. **Nigel Gibbs**

Key Facts

UK Arrival
June 2002
Newport Docks
MV 'Jumbo Vision'

Built
2002
EMD plant, London, Ontario, Canada

Livery
From New :
Blue with Orange cantrail and solebar stripes; orange cabs

March 2015 :
Turquoise and Blue.
Grey stripe and Aggregate Industries logo.

Names
July 2015 'Sence'

No.66711 (top right) is seen passing Albany Park on the Dartford - Lewisham line, 25th April, hauling Class 465 EMU No.465249 in between two 'barrier' vehicles, running as 5X89, the 11:58 Slade Green Depot - Doncaster Wabtec on this occasion.   **Ian Cuthbertson**

On 25th June, Aggregate Industries liveried No.66711 (below) powers 6E84, the 08:20 (TWThO) Middleton Towers - Monk Bretton loaded sand train along the ECML, having just emerged from the north portal of Stoke Tunnel.

The tunnel is 880 yards long and, at 345ft above sea level, is the highest point on the ECML between London King's Cross and Berwick upon Tweed.   **Jamie Squibbs**

Key Facts

Built	La Grange, Illinois, USA		
Completed	December 1985		
Shipping Details	Shipping Port	: Newport News, Virginia, USA	
	Ship	: MV. 'Fairlift'	
	Sailing Date	: 8th January 1986	
	Arrival Date	: 21st January 1986	
	Arrival Port	: Southampton	
In Traffic	December 1985	: (UK)	
	June 2015	: (UK)	
Allocations / Owner	From new	: Foster Yeoman	59003
	May 1998	: DB Cargo, Germany	259 003 - 2
	May 2000	: Heavy Haul Power International	259 003 - 2
	August 2014	**: GBRf**	**59003**
Name	June 1986	: 'Yeoman Highlander'	
Livery	From New	: (UK) Foster Yeoman Silver with blue bands / FY logo on body side	
	May 1998	: (Germany) Red & Blue with DB Cargo and Foster Yeoman logo	
	May 2000	: (Germany) Red & Blue with HHPI branding	
	May 2015	**: (UK) GBRf Blue with Orange**	

YEOMAN HIGHLANDER

59003 **'Yeoman Highlander'** (above) is seen out & about for the first time on 29th May after a lengthy spell inside Eastleigh works being overhauled and rectified for use in the UK after life in Germany. It is stabled at Guildford during its test run; 0Z60, Eastleigh - Guildford - Eastleigh, prior to going to the West Somerset Railway to attend their 'Mixed Traffic Weekend'. **Mark Pike**

(inset) : 'Yeoman Highlander' nameplate. **Mark Thomas**

Less than a month after the commencement of Foster Yeoman Class 59 operations in this country, the as yet unnamed No. **59003** (above) passes Fairwood Junction with the 10:03hrs Merehead - Eastleigh stone train on 11th March 1986. Unthinkable politically in the 1960s, the purchase of US designed locomotives in preference to British built designs was to gain momentum, resulting in the situation twenty years later, when virtually all freight locos in the UK were foreign built. The tracks in the foreground are the Westbury avoiding lines, while the train is on the original main line, as it will run round in Westbury Yard, in order to gain the former Southern Railway route via Salisbury. **Martin Loader**

No.**59003** returns from Germany, shipped to the UK via the Port of Immingham. In miserable weather, Class 47/8 No.47815 'Great Western' tows No.59003 (below) over the River Don at Sandall Lock on 13th October 2014, running as 0Z59, the 11:00 Immingham - Eastleigh. The train is booked at Barrow Hill between 13:46hrs - 14:06hrs, where the 47 is due to come off in favour of a pair of GBRf Class 20s for the remainder of the journey. **Alan Padley**

Key Facts

Built	BREL, Doncaster
Introduced	August 1980
First Depot	Tinsley TMD
Livery	BR Blue, followed by:
	Two-Tone Grey
	Two-Tone Grey with Coal Sector Decals
	Trainload Grey
	EWS Maroon & Gold
	Fertis Grey with *fertis* logo
	UKRL Dark Grey
Withdrawn	September 2006
Return To Traffic	**November 2014**

Notes

(1) 01/07/2005 - 27/09/2006 : 56081 hired to Fertis in France for infrastructure work.

(2) November 2013 : UK Rail Leasing purchase No.56081 from DBS.

(3) November 2014 : 56081 hired to Freightliner, as 'super shunter' at Crewe, Basford Hall Yard.

From this ..... in original BR Blue livery, No.**56081** (above) stands outside Toton TMD's main maintenance building. Note the last three digits of its running number under the horn box.   **Ian Cuthbertson**

(inset) : Looking resplendent in its new livery, No.**56081** is seen parked up at UKRL's Leicester depot on 14th May, along with Class 37/9 No.37906, which is on the fuelling point.

The former EWS fuelling and stabling point at Leicester is now the operational base of UKRL (UK Rail Leasing Company) where their locos are being kept. Along with No.56081, UKRL acquired further 'Grids' from DBS: Nos.56007, 56009, 56018, 56031, 56032, 56037, 56038, 56060, 56065, 56069, 56077, 56098, 56104, and 56106.   **Craig Adamson**

To this .... some 35 years later and the newly-returned to traffic 'grid" makes its revenue-earning debut on the main line, 23rd June, hired by FHH to DBS to work the Willesden - Calvert spoil train; a turn often contracted to a DCR Class 56.

On 9th July, UK Rail Leasing's No.**56081** (above) looks superb as it rounds the curve near North Lee with 6Z57, the 10:16 Calvert - Willesden Euro Terminal spoil empties. The train actually left Calvert nearly half an hour early but, due to pathing constraints on this single track line between Aylesbury and Princes Risborough, it had to wait for the passage of 2P37, the 10:33 Aylesbury - Princes Risborough DMU, before it could continue south.   **Martin Loader**

On the second day of operations, 24th June, No.**56081** (below) heads 6Z57 making its way into the Capital at Ealing Broadway, which is a western terminus for two London Underground lines; the District line from Upminster and the Central line from Epping.   **Mark Pike**

Two Tone Grey

During the '90s, Freightliner hired four Class 56s to work 'liners between Ipswich Yard and Felixstowe; apparently, the branch was too steeply graded for a single Class 47. The locos were outbased at Ipswich and the Lawley Street and Wilton freightliners were worked throughout by a single 56.

No.56081 (above) is seen leaving the Felixstowe branch at Westerfield on 30th April 1996 with an unidentified freightliner service, passing the signal box which closed in 1999, when signalling came under the control of Colchester Power Signal Box.   **Ian Cuthbertson**

This is just like old times, when Class 56s were once a common sight working MGR coal trains in Yorkshire. No.56081 (below) passes Burton Salmon with a Gascoigne Wood - Tyne Dock loaded MGR train (circa. 1990), running via Castleford in order to turn the train. This stretch of track was probably the busiest MGR route on the network with a constant procession of coal trains running between Gascoigne Wood / Tyne Dock / Immingham to Drax, Eggborough and Ferrybridge power stations.   **Ian Ball**

For a time, No.56081 was allocated to the Railfreight coal sector and had the appropriate Black & Yellow coal decals applied to the body side.

No.56081 (top right) takes a well earned weekend break at Knottingley, before resuming Aire Valley MGR coal duties on the Monday, moving coal to either Drax, Eggborough or Ferrybridge PS. **Ian Cuthbertson**

Two Tone Grey - Coal Sector

During the English, Scottish & Welsh Railways era, many locos received this corporate livery.

No.56081 (middle) is heading through Hatfield & Stainforth station on 26th October 1999 with 6M07, 10:45 Roxby - Pendleton empty GMC 'Binliner'. **Neil Harvey**

EWS Maroon & Gold

The LGV Est, high speed line between Paris and Strasbourg, opened in 2007 and 26 Class 56s were hired to Fertis by EWS to work ballast trains on this line.

Once back in the UK, No.56081 (right) spent time at Old Oak Common awaiting a decision on its future. **Jamie Squibbs**

Fertis Grey

Key Facts

Built	Brush Traction, Loughborough
Introduced	April 1960
Depot	Washwood Heath

Numbers

31601	: March 1999
31186	: December 1973
D5609	: From new

Livery   **Devon & Cornwall Grey**, previously:

BR Green with DCR / British American Railway Services Branding.

FM Rail (Fragonset) Cerise Pink.

New Railtrack Blue & Lime Green.

Fragonset Black, Red body side band, Silver roof.

BR Civil Engineer's Yellow and Grey 'Dutch' livery.

BR Blue

BR Green with White body side stripe

Names

'Devon Diesel Society'	: May 2015
'Gauge 'O' Guild 1956 - 2006'	: September 2006
'The Mayor of Casterbridge'	: October 2004
'Bletchley Park 'Station X''	: March 1999

DCR Grey Livery : No.31601 was repainted into the latest DCR grey livery by volunteers from the Devon Diesel Society. As a thank you, the loco was named after the society in a short ceremony at Buckfastleigh station on Friday, 22nd May, before working passenger and freight services during the South Devon Railway's 1960s gala that was laid on during that weekend.

Here, No.31601 (above) is seen posing for the camera at Buckfastleigh.   **Robert Sherwood**

Under the cover of darkness, No.**31601 'Devon Diesel Society'** (above) sits at Eastleigh on 18th June with 6086, Willesden - Eastleigh wagon move; the wagon is a 'Murco' branded 'TEA' 100ton Bogie Petroleum Tank, numbered in the GERS 89001 - GERS 89028 range, built in 2001 by Arbel Fauvet, France. The wagon is going for repair at Eastleigh works.   **Simon Howard**

Flashback .... the first of six images of this particular loco in post-BR Blue livery ....

Yellow & Grey 'Dutch'

Before conversion to Class 31/6 sub-class and the addition of ETS (Electric Train Supply), No.**31186** (below) is seen stabled at March along with sister No.31187, both sporting the civil engineer's 'dutch' Yellow & Grey livery. Note the cast BR double arrows logo under the cab of No.31186.   **Ian Ball**

31601
'Bletchley Park 'Station X''
Fragonset Black

Adorned in Fragonset Black livery with Red body side band, No.31601 (above) is seen at Crewe Works on 21st May 2000. Fragonset, formed in 1997, initially purchased four Class 47/7 locos for hire, followed by several redundant Class 31 locos from EWS in 1998.

New Railtrack Blue & Lime Green

Fragonset had several customers, including Virgin Trains, WCRC and New Railtrack, who all regularly hired in Class 31s to cover shortages. No.31601 (below), still carrying 'Bletchley Park 'Station X'' nameplates, stands at Westbury on 12th July 2003 wearing New Railtrack Blue & Lime Green livery.   **Simon Howard (2)**

'Gauge 'O' Guild 1956-2006'

No.**31601**, top 'n' tailed with No.31106 (top right) passes Oakley, east of Battledown, on the Basingstoke - Salisbury main line (7th May 2008) with 1Z11, the 09:41 Eastleigh RC - Salisbury CHS.

A test coach is sandwiched between the two 'Peds', while undertaking track recording duties.   **Simon Howard**

'The Mayor of Casterbridge'

Wessex Trains hired Class 31s to haul passenger services between Bristol T. Meads and Brighton / Weymouth.

These services ceased in 2004, but Wessex Trains continued to use 31s on special trains, until 2006, when Fragonset folded.

Now carrying a new name ('The Mayor of Casterbridge'), No.**31601** (middle) is seen leaving Weston-super-Mare on 19th June 2005 with ECS bound for Bristol, following a C4 Concert on the beach special train. InterCity liveried Another 'Ped', No.31454 'The heart of Wessex' is on the rear of the train.   **Chris Perkins**

Cerise Pink

DCR Green

No.31601 was acquired by DCR (Devon and Cornwall Railways (DCR), a British freight operating company subsidiary of BARS (British American Railway Services).

The Company repainted three locos (31452/31601/56303) in BR Green livery.

On 20th September 2014, No.**31601** (right) approaches Basingstoke with No.31452, running light engine to the engineer's sidings at Totton (0Z31) to collect a 'RailVac' for their next turn of duty.

                    Simon Howard

Key Facts

Built	: English Electric Vulcan Foundry, Newton Le Willows	
In Traffic	: February 1965	
First Depot	: Darnall, Sheffield (39B / DA)	
Numbers	: **37401**	(01/1985)
	37268	(02/1974)
	D6968	(02/1965)
Livery	: **BR Blue, Large Logo**	(07/2015)
	Royal Scotsman Maroon	(03/2001)
	EWS Maroon & Gold	(1998)
	Railfreight Two Tone Grey	(1990)
	BR InterCity Mainline	(08/1988)
	BR Blue, Large Logo	(06/1985)
	BR Blue	(?)
	BR Brunswick Green	(02/1965)
Names	: **'Mary Queen of Scots'**	(11/1995)
	: 'The Royal Scotsman'	(03/2001)
	: 'Mary Queen of Scots'	(11/1985)
Withdrawn	: March 2013	
Reinstated	: July 2015	

No.37401 'Mary Queen of Scots' (above / inset) at Carlisle Kingmoor. 18th July.   **Mark Thomas (2)**

BR Blue, Large Logo

30 years separate this photograph and the one opposite ..... No.**37401** (above), resplendent in BR Blue Large Logo livery, with body side white 'Scottie Dog' emblem, poses for the camera during its attendance at Haymarket TMD open day in July 1985.

In May 1984, the then No.37268 entered Crewe works for conversion to a Class 37/4. Following a protracted period, the loco finally emerged and worked the Crewe Works Test Train to & from Llandudno Junction on 19th June 1985. It became No.37401 and moved to Scotland. **John Chalcraft**

'Mary Queen of Scots'

Railfreight Two Tone Grey

On a dull 11th August 1997, No.37401 'Mary Queen of Scots' (below) approaches County March Summit, near Tyndrum Upper, in typical West Highland weather with 1Y11, the 05:05 Edinburgh Waverley - Fort William ScotRail sleeper. This is a portion off the overnight sleeper from London Euston. **Martin Loader**

37401
'Retro'

'Mary Queen of Scots' EWS Maroon & Gold

Looking superb in its new EWS livery, No.**37401 'Mary Queen of Scots'** + No.37225 (above) pass Berkley (Frome) on 19th August 1998, with 7Z87, the 07:45 Merehead - Exeter Riverside loaded stone service. The 'tractors' are heading for Westbury for a reversal, before heading off for Devon. **John Chalcraft**

The 'Royal Scotsman' Royal Scotsman Maroon

On 11 June 2005, No.**37401 'The Royal Scotsman'** (above) arrives at the western end of Loch Eilt on the Fort William to Mallaig line heading 1Z18, the 05:32 SRPS Kilmarnock - Mallaig 'West Highlander' railtour. The loco makes a fine sight as it emerges from the woods with its matching rake of maroon stock, on a day when the sunshine is sadly conspicuous by its absence, but at least it's not raining! **Martin Loader**

BR InterCity Mainline

On 23rd September 1988, No.**37401 'Mary Queen of Scots'** (above) crosses Loch Awe with the local afternoon service to Dalmally, running as 2Y92, the 15:40hrs from Oban. The loco had earlier worked into Oban with 1Y13, the 12:20hrs ex-Glasgow Queen Street.

During their time in Scotland, the Class 37/4s also worked freight services over the West Highland Line as illustrated here. On 4th November 1988, No.**37401 'Mary Queen of Scots'** (below) arrives at Taynuilt with 7D09, the 09:30 Oban - Mossend Yard 'Speedlink' service, which includes discharged 2-axle fuel oil tanks from Oban and Connel Ferry. **John Chalcraft (2)**

Key Facts

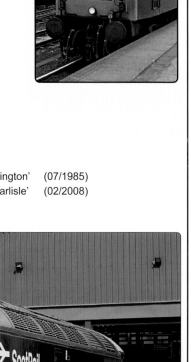

Built	Brush Falcon Works
Introduced	August 1966
First Depot	London Midland Western Lines (Birmingham Division)
Numbers	D1948 (08/1966)
	47505 (02/1974)
	47712 (11/1979)
Livery	**ScotRail Black & White Bands,**
	with Saltire Blue Stripe, previously:
	DRS Blue, Compass Logo
	FMR 'Blue Pullman'
	Fragonset Black with Red Stripe
	Waterman Black
	ReS Dark Grey and Red with Blue Markings
	ScotRail Black & White Bands with Saltire Blue Stripe
	BR Monastral Blue, Large Logo
	BR Monastral Blue
	BR Two Tone Green

Names	'Lady Diana Spencer'	(04/1981)	'Dick Whittington'	(07/1985)
	'Artemis'	(01/2001)	'Pride of Carlisle'	(02/2008)

Status	**Preserved**

ScotRail Black & White Bands, Blue Stripe : The preserved Class 47/7 No.47712 (above) stands outside Carlisle Kingmoor depot on 18th July in former ScotRail colours.

The loco was purchased by the Crewe Diesel Preservation Group (CDPG) in 2013, after becoming surplus to Direct Rail Services requirements. Initially based at the Crewe Heritage Centre, it moved to the Weardale Railway where it was restored to full working condition as displayed at Carlisle Kingmoor

(inset) : **BR Blue** : Close up view of the front end of the unnamed No.47712, as it awaits departure from Glasgow Queen Street on 1st April 1980 with the 11.30hrs service to Edinburgh Waverley. Journey time then was 47 minutes with only the one stop at Haymarket to set down!   **Jim Ramsay**

Black & White Nostalgia

Under the wires on the ECML and prior to Class 47/7 status, No.47505 (above) accelerates out of Gasworks Tunnel on 7th April 1978 with the 17:10 King's Cross - Hull. At the time, No.47505 was allocated to Landore TMD, Swansea, and remained so until its transfer to Haymarket TMD in September 1979.   **John Chalcraft**

No.47712 was named 'Lady Diana Spencer' at Glasgow Queen Street station by Sir Peter Parker, Chairman of the BRB, on 30th April 1981, . Interestingly, 'Prince Charles Edward' plates were fitted during a visit to Crewe Works in August 1980 but were removed in October before No.47712 returned to service.

ScotRail blue-stripe livery was applied during overhaul at Crewe Works in early 1985 and was carried until overhaul at Doncaster in 1991. On 30th May 1988, No.47712 'Lady Diana Spencer' (below), in ScotRail livery, passes Linlithgow with the 14.30 Glasgow Queen Street - Edinburgh Waverley.   **Brian Morrison**

ReS Dark Grey and Red

The former parcels sector Class 47/7, No.47712 'Lady Diana Spencer' (above), passes South Moreton on 18th August 1991 with 1B29, the 13:40 London Paddington - Hereford service, having been recently transferred to the NWRA Thames Valley passenger pool.   **Martin Loader**

BR Blue

On 5th April 1980, an unnamed No.47712 (below) in ubiquitous BR Blue livery, is seen stabled at Edinburgh Waverley, in between 'push-pull' duties to and from Glasgow Queen Street. In the late 1970s, British Rail decided to convert twelve Class 47/4s to operate the Glasgow - Edinburgh service to increase speed and reliability. The locos became 47/7s and were fitted with TDM push-pull equipment, long-range fuel tanks, and maintained to operate at 100 mph. The conversions began in 1979.   **Fred Kerr**

BR Blue, Large Logo

The twelve converted Class 47s (Nos.47701 - 47712) are probably best remembered on 'push-pull' duties between Glasgow Queen Street and Edinburgh Waverley. They replaced the unreliable Class 27s on this circuit from 1980.

In 1985, 'push-pull' services spread to the Aberdeen route.

On 15th October 1981, No.47712 'Lady Diana Spencer' (right) in BR Blue Large Logo livery passes the former Elliot Junction, Arbroath, with the 11:55hrs Aberdeen - Glasgow Queen Street service.   **Brian Livie**

Lady Diana Spencer

In the 'classic' setting of Princes Street Gardens, Edinburgh, No.47712 'Lady Diana Spencer' (below) dodges the shadows on 31st May 1984, with another 'shuttle' service from Glasgow Queen Street.

From a historical perspective, the Edinburgh and Glasgow Railway company constructed a sunken railway line in 1846 along the southern edge of Princes Street Gardens to connect Haymarket with a new General Station adjoining the North British Railway Company's North Bridge Edinburgh terminus, both stations later being named Waverley.

This involved building Haymarket Tunnel (separate north and south tunnels), 1,040 yards long, between the western end of the gardens and Haymarket Station. A shorter tunnel (again, two separate tunnels, 130 yards long) was also dug through the Mound dividing the East and West Gardens.   **Fred Kerr**

'Artemis'
Fragonset Black with Red Stripe

No.47712 'Artemis' (left) strums alongside the Exe estuary at Cockwood, near Starcross, on Sunday, 9th September 2001, with 1C52, the 14:03 Paddington - Penzance. **Peter Slater**

'Dick Whittington'
Waterman Black

On 18th May 1998, No.47712 (middle) approaches Wolvercote Junction, north Oxford, with 1M79, 16:47 Reading - Liverpool Lime Street Virgin XC service.

No.47712 allegedly carried 'Dick Whittington' nameplates from 1995 until 2000. However, there clearly isn't a plate on this side of the loco in this picture!

On 2nd June 1996, No.47712 'Dick Whittington' (below) enters Taffs Well station with a 'vice-DMU' service from Merthyr Tydfil to Barry Island. Sadly, the distinctive GWR centre pivot signal has long gone.

The Heritage style nameplates were unveiled on 5th July 1995 at London Liverpool Street station by the Lord Mayor of London. **Martin Loader (2)**

'Artemis'

BR Blue Pullman

Along with No.47709, No.47712 carried the 'Blue Pullman' livery. No.47712 'Artemis' (above) hurries northbound through Colchester leading the 'Queen of Scots' charter rake, forming 1Z83, the 10:50 London Victoria - Cambridge. The train ran via the North London Line, the Great Eastern Main Line and Dullingham to reach Cambridge. Classmate No.47832 tails the antique stock.   **James Welham**

'Pride of Carlisle'

DRS Compass Logo

The present day .... No.47712 is now in DRS Blue livery with Compass logo, complete with 'Pride of Carlisle' nameplates, which it received in February 2008. No.47712 'Pride of Carlisle' (below) is seen posing for the camera at Eastleigh Works Open Day on 23rd May 2009.   **Richard Jones**

'Forth 125'

1890 - 2015

4th March 1890

Background

4th March 2015 marks the *125th Anniversary* of the opening of the Forth Rail Bridge in **1890**, which has now been granted **World Heritage status**.

The Forth Bridge is a cantilever design, spanning the Firth of Forth, the mid point of which is some 11.50 miles west of Edinburgh Waverley station. It opened on 4 March 1890 by the Prince of Wales (later King Edward VII), who drove a final gold plated rivet into the structure.

The bridge leaves Edinburgh at South Queensferry and arrives in Fife at North Queensferry and, until 1917, when the Quebec Bridge was completed in Canada, the Forth Bridge had the longest single cantilever bridge span in the world.

Design & Construction

The Bill for constructing the bridge was passed in May 1882 and, in December of that year, the contract was given to Sir Thomas Tancred, Mr. T. H. Falkiner and Mr. Joseph Philips, civil engineers and contractor, and Sir William Arrol & Co..

The cantilever bridge was designed by Sir John Fowler and Sir Benjamin Baker and has three double cantilevers with two 1,710ft suspended spans between them. As required by the Admiralty, the rail level has a clearance of 150ft above high water.

This is a magnificent sight, the Forth Rail Bridge, the Forth Road Bridge and the new road crossing under construction, all in one vista. On the second day of DRS operating the 'Fife Circle' commuter services, No.**68006 'Daring'** (above), complete with matching ScotRail set of coaches, crosses the Forth Bridge in early morning sunshine, hauling 2K18, 07:35 Cardenden - Edinburgh Waverley.   **Guy Houston**

It's 17:45hrs in the evening on 13th April 2010, BR Standard Class 7 4-6-2 Pacific No.**70013 'Oliver Cromwell'** (opposite) is about to leave the Forth Bridge with 1Z49, the 09:23 Inverness - Edinburgh leg of 'Great Britain III'; the tour having left Inverness behind 'Oliver Cromwell' and LNER K4 Class 2-6-0 No.61994 'The Great Marquess'. The 'Brit' is working solo from Dundee.   **John Whitehouse**

1890 - 2015

On 3rd September 2013, FHH Class 66/6 No.**66607** *(above)* crosses the Forth Rail Bridge just before sunset with 6B32, the 16:52 Aberdeen - Oxwellmains empty cement tanks - a beautiful composition!
Steven Brykajlo

DBS liveried Class 66/0 No.**66114** *(below)* is seen having crossed the cantilever section of the Bridge on 10th June 2014 at North Queensferry with 6X88, the 05:38 Hartlepool - Georgemas Junction pipe train.
Steven Brykajlo

(above) : An unusual view of the Forth Rail Bridge photographed from sea level. As a small coastal vessel passes a moored cruise ship, an East Coast HST crosses the Bridge with 1S11, the 10:00 King's Cross - Aberdeen service on 25th July 2014. **Mark Pike**

(below): The flood lights which illuminate the Forth Railway Bridge reflect in the exhaust of 'Princess Coronation' Pacific No.**46233 'Duchess of Sutherland'**. She is working the final leg of the afternoon SRPS 'Forth Circle' charter (1Z30, 15:20 Dalmeny - Inverkeithing) across the Firth of Forth on 14th September 2014. In the background is the Forth Road Bridge, which celebrated it's 50th anniversary the day before, while beyond it are the central supporting pillars of the new Forth road crossing, presently under construction and scheduled for completion in 2016. **John Whitehouse**

(above) : DBS Class 67 No.**67026 'Diamond Jubilee'** is seen crossing the Forth Rail Bridge above North Queensferry on the evening of 1st July 2014, while working 2K14, the 18:15 Glenrothes - Edinburgh Waverley 'Fife Circle' service.
Steven Brykajlo

(below) : DRS Class 37/6 No.**37601** hauls 1Q13, Craigentinny - Craigentinny test train over the Forth Rail Bridge on 8th April 2014 and is seen approaching North Queensferry. In the background is the Forth Road bridge, which carries the A90 from Edinburgh, opened by Queen Elizabeth II and the Duke of Edinburgh on 4th September 1964, at which time the centuries-old ferry service was discontinued. It is 8,241ft long and has a central main span of 3,301ft, two side spans of 1,339ft and the approach viaducts are 827ft on the north side and 1,437ft on the south side.
Alastair Blackwood

Design & Construction (continued)

The Forth Rail bridge is 8,296ft in length and carries double track.

The bridge consists of two main spans of 1,710ft and the length of the bridge is 5,348ft between portals with 15 approach spans leading to the portals; 10 to the south portal and 5 to the north portal.

The weight of the bridge superstructure was 50,513 tonnes and 6.5 million rivets were used during its construction, plus 640,000 cubic feet of granite.

The three great four-tower cantilever structures are 330ft tall and rest on separate granite piers, which are known as (from south to north) Queensferry pier, Inchgarvie pier and Fife pier. Each of the towers has four steel tubes 12ft in diameter and reach a height of 361ft above high water; the foundations extend 89ft below this into the river bed.

Painting the Bridge

"Painting the Forth Bridge" is a colloquial expression for a never-ending task, coined on the erroneous belief that repainting was required and commenced immediately upon completion of the previous repaint. Such a practice never existed!

Work started in 2002 to fully repaint the bridge for the first time in its history - the contract, worth £130 million, was awarded to Balfour Beatty and was completed in December 2011.

Up to 4,000 tonnes of scaffolding was on the bridge at any time and all previous layers of paint were removed using copper slag fired at up to 200 miles per hour, which exposed the steel and allowed any repairs to be made. The paint was specifically developed for the bridge by Leigh Paints, derived from that used in the North Sea oil industry, and 53,000 gallons of paint was applied to 2,740,000 sq ft of the structure.

It is not expected to need repainting for at least 20 years.

(above) : Inchgarvie (also known as 'Inch Garvie') is a small, uninhabited, island in the Firth of Forth and its name comes from Innis Garbhach which is Scottish Gaelic for "rough island". On the rocks around the island sit four caissons that make up the foundations of the Forth Bridge.

Although now uninhabited, Inchgarvie has been inhabited throughout various periods of history, dating back to the late 15th century, and was strategically important; the remains of the fort are still visible. Like nearby Inchmickery, its profile and colour make it look like a battleship from a distance and it was used for gun placements during World War 1 and 2.

Looking across the island on Sunday, 17th April 2011, a plume of exhaust drift away from LMS Royal Scot 4-6-0 No.**46115 'Scots Guardsman'** as it heads onto the bridge at Dalmeny with 1Z28, the 09:44 Edinburgh - Inverness on the second day of the 'Great Britain IV' tour. Note the protective cladding placed on the Bridge, while repainting and repairs are carried out. **John Whitehouse**

(Opposite) : Under a darkening sky, DBS Class 60 No.**60009** comes off the Forth Rail Bridge into Dalmeny on 12th March 2008 working 6D71, Linkswood - Mossend empty aviation fuel tanks. This train is now operated by Colas Rail and bypasses the Bridge by using the Dunfermline - Kincardine - Alloa - Stirling route, which opened fully in 2008. **Steven Brykajlo**

'Solar Eclipse'

Introduction

Solar eclipses occur in cycles, about every 18 years, and can be a spectacular sight.

This is when the Moon passes between Earth and the Sun, thereby totally or partly obscuring the image of the Sun for a viewer on Earth. The Moon's apparent diameter will appear to be larger than the Sun's, blocking all direct sunlight, turning day into darkness.

This particular eclipse is the same day as the Vernal Equinox, 20th March. The track of totality passes across the North Atlantic and into the Arctic Ocean and the only populated places from which the totality could be seen are the Faroe Islands and Svalbard (Norway).

Images

So, on this day, here is a small selection of images by contributors, who were out recording the passage of trains, as well as the eclipse, on this special day in March.

20th March

DENCHWORTH : DBS 'Drax' Class 60 No.60066 (above) passes Denchworth on the GWML ('Down Relief') with 6B33, the 13:00 Theale Murco - Robeston Sidings discharged bogie tanks.   **Nigel Gibbs**

BARNBY DUN : The first Class 66/0 to receive DBS corporate colours is No.66152 (top right) and this loco is seen passing Barnby Dun with 6H62, the 08:51 Immingham - Drax loaded biomass. The consist is purpose-built covered hoppers, manufactured by W H Davis, and carry a 'IIAD' carkind, within a 70.0698.001-0 to 70.0698.175-2 number range.   **Alan Padley**

EASTREA : GBRf's Class 66/7, No.66770 (opposite, middle), is pictured making good time at Eastrea (between March and Whittlesea) leading a fully laden 4Z33, the 11:22 Felixstowe South - Doncaster Railport Intermodal. The 'Zulu' headcode, instead of the usual 4E33, reflects that this service now travels to Doncaster along the 'joint line' via Spalding, Lincoln and Gainsborough.   **James Welham**

GILBERDYKE : BR Blue Large Logo Class 47/4 No.47847 (bottom right) looks great passing Gilberdyke with 4D94, the 10:30 Doncaster Down Decoy - Hull Coal Terminal loaded gypsum. This loco's first 'meaningful work' for a number of years, after long periods in store at Eastleigh, took place on 11th March, when it double-headed 4D93, the 09:41 Doncaster - Drax gypsum with another Class 47 hired-in from Riviera trains, No.47843 'Vulcan'.   **Pauline McKenna**

189

The Eclipse

20th March : For many viewers across the land, the day was miserable with a lot of cloud, although the clouds certainly make it slightly easier to see and photograph the eclipse. This is a view taken from a garden in Hull, apparently, cloudless and full sun south of the River Humber at the time!

Syd Young

'The Three Queens'

25th May : The 175th Anniversary of the founding of the Cunard Line is celebrated by three days of events between 24th – 26th May 2015. Without question, the highlight is the assembly of all three current Cunard 'Queens' in Liverpool for just a few hours on 25th May; Queen Mary 2 (centre) is joined by her sister ships, 'Queen Elizabeth' (on the left) and 'Queen Victoria' (on the right). They are lined abreast in the Mersey Estuary with the traditional fire ship, whose hoses are in full flow. To complete the scene, the RAF's 'Red Arrows' display team streak across the sky above the liners.
John Whitehouse

'Cunard 175'

1840 - 2015

Introduction

Cunard's Three Queens - RMS 'Queen Mary 2', MS 'Queen Elizabeth' and MS 'Queen Victoria' visit the Port of Liverpool between 24th - 26th May to celebrate the 175th anniversary of the famous shipping line.

The River Mersey hosts a fantastic water ballet by the iconic ships as part of the celebrations, with over 1 million people lining the quayside on both sides of the Mersey to witness this historic event, honouring the birth of Cunard in Liverpool.

The Three Queens	Length (Ft)	Gross Tonnage
Queen Mary 2	1,132	148,528
Queen Elizabeth	965	90,901
Queen Victoria	964.5	90,000

Portfolio

Here is a small selection of images to illustrate this unique event. However, poor weather on the day deterred many photographers from venturing out, so there's only a couple of railway images on offer.

(Above) : After the various line-ups between Liverpool and Birkenhead pier heads on 25th May, the three 'Queens' then go their separate ways. 'Queen Mary 2' departs from Cunard's spiritual home bound for St. Petersburg, while 'Queen Elizabeth' manoeuvres into the cruise liner terminal at Liverpool Pier Head.

In the background are Liverpool's 'Three Graces': The Royal Liver Building, the Cunard Building and the Port of Liverpool Building, the latter with its distinctive dome. The former is probably the most famous, due mainly to the presence of a 'liver-bird' perched on the top of each colonnade.   **John Whitehouse**

25 MAY

As you can see, it all looks pretty gloomy at Bescot, where GBRf Class 66/7 No.66721 'Harry Beck' (above) is stabled in between duties. The loco will next work 6F16, the 04:58 Bescot - Stud Farm empty ballast box wagons.   **Craig Adamson**

Further north, overcast weather conditions also prevail, at Sherburn-in-Elmet. Ex-Fertis Class 56 'grid', No.56103 (below), looking pretty shabby externally, passes with 6Z35, the 09:00 Chaddesden Sidings - Stockton (Thompson) with a rake of empty 'JRAs'. These bogie box wagons have been strengthened by the addition of an all-round trim to the top of the wagon.   **Pauline McKenna**

Cunard - Timeline

5th February 1840 : RMS 'Britannia' is launched.

Samuel Cunard simply wanted a ship to carry passengers and mail and bring them *'safely over and safely back'*. The Britannia carried 115 first class passengers, 86 crew, 600 tons of coal, the Atlantic mail, chickens, a cow to provide fresh milk and three cats to keep down rats.

25th July 1855 : RMS 'China' launched; Cunard's first iron-hulled transatlantic vessel and the largest ship afloat.

1st January 1862 : Maiden voyage of RMS 'China', Cunard's first propeller-driven ship

28th April 1865 : Sir Samuel Cunard dies

25th June 1884 : RMS 'Umbria' launched, fitted with two tall funnels and the last ship to carry sails.

7th June 1906 : RMS 'Lusitania' launched, a 'Monarch of the Sea'.

20th September 1906 : RMS 'Mauretania' launched.

21st April 1913 : RMS 'Aquitania launched, survived a collision with an iceberg and a torpedo hit.

15th April 1915 : RMS 'Carpathia' rescues all 866 survivors from RMS.'Titanic'.

7th May 1915 : Sinking of RMS 'Lusitania'.

Seven days after leaving New York for Liverpool, with 1,959 passengers and crew onboard, a single torpedo fired from German U-boat No.U-20 hit the starboard side of the Lusitania, just off the southern coast of Ireland.

The ship sunk in just 18 seconds and only 761 of those on board were rescued.

1st January 1916 : Cunard Building in Liverpool completed

18th November 1919 : RMS 'Mauretania' sails from Southampton, Cunard's new main departure point.

21st November 1922 :   RMS 'Laconia II' becomes the first passenger liner ever to go on a world cruise

26th September 1934 : HM Queen Mary launches RMS 'Queen Mary', first Monarch to launch a merchant ship.

27th September 1938 : HM Queen Elizabeth launches RMS 'Queen Elizabeth', then the largest liner ever built.

9th August 1968 : HM The Queen launches RMS 'Queen Elizabeth 2' (QE2).

12th May 1982 : The QE2 carries 6,000 troops to the Falklands, during the conflict with Argentina.

8th January 2004 : HM The Queen launches RMS 'Queen Mary 2'.

10th December 2007 : HRH The Duchess of Cornwall names MS 'Queen Victoria'.

The first Cunard liner not to carry mail, hence no 'RMS' designation.

11th October 2010 : HM The Queen names MS 'Queen Elizabeth'.

1st January 2015 - 31st December 2015 : Cunard's 175th Anniversary worldwide celebrations.

Cunard 175: the 'Queens'

A leaden sky greets the Cunard Liners 'Queen Elizabeth' and 'Queen Victoria' on 25th May, as they join their big sister 'Queen Mary 2' (QM2), which had arrived in Liverpool the previous day. QM2 then slipped her mooring at the city's ocean terminal to make her way out of the River Mersey to greet her sisters' arrival. The three liners (top left) then formed into line astern, with 'Queen Elizabeth' leading, to sail into the Mersey as the main Cunard 175 event. The meeting point was at the Brazil Buoy, at the head of the deep water channel leading into the Mersey.

On the day, the three 'Queens' execute a delicate, carefully choreographed, 90 degree turn to starboard so that the ships are positioned facing out from the Cunard Building, next to the Liver Building, on Liverpool's quayside. 'Queen Elizabeth' leads the turn, followed by 'Queen Victoria' and then 'QM2'. In a narrow channel, manoeuvering three ships with a combined weight of around 330,000 gross tonnes in such a confined space must have been tricky, to say the least.   **John Whitehouse (3)**

Finally, viewed from River Park, Port Sunlight, the turn has been completed and the three 'Queens' (from left to right) 'Queen Elizabeth', 'Queen Victoria' and the 'Queen Mary 2', are now positioned in the River Mersey, 90 degrees facing out from the Liverpool quayside.   **Colin Partington**

"The Light At The End Of The Tunnel"

These days, china clay trains on the Par - Newquay branch are thin on the ground, perhaps, as few as one a day. So, making a round trip of more than 200 miles, with no guarantee of sunshine nor seeing one of these trains, and all for a 'shed,' is devotion indeed. Was it worth it, you can judge for yourself ....

A work-stained Class 66/0 No.66078 (below) sees daylight as it emerges from the 52 yards long Luxulyan Tunnel with a rake of empty 'CDA' 2-axle china clay hoppers, running as 6G07, the 13.50 Fowey Dock (Carne Point) - Goonbarrow Junction. Note the cladding to prevent rock fall in the cutting.   **Peter Slater**

"Tired Of Hanging Around"
(opposite)

No time to hang around here, unloading commences shortly after the train comes to a halt.

Seen beneath one of the huge container cranes at Freightliner's Southampton Maritime Terminal (FLT), Class 70 No.70018 slowly draws in with 4O54, the 06:12hrs service from Leeds. In this shot the crane driver can be seen in the cab (vertigo sufferers need not apply!) along with the Peninsular & Orient (P & O) MV 'Arcadia' berthed at Southampton Cruise Ship Terminal. For the record ....

1. MV 'Arcadia' is 951 ft long, 84,342 tons and was launched in June 2004.

2. The crane at the FLT has a span of 151ft with an operational outreach of 85ft, capable of spanning 13 lanes with a lift height of just under 56ft. The respective parts in view are the 'Boom' at the top, under which a 'Trolley' moves across it and the 'Cab' is affixed to a 'Rotator'; the yellow bit is the 'Spreader' whose components are designed to withstand a 30G impact.   **David Hayes**

(above)

"Physical Graffiti"

A 153 yard long wall at the perimeter of Seven Oaks Park in Grangetown (Cardiff) is full of colourful surprises. Adorned with legal graffiti, the wall supports the railway and is owned by Network Rail. Street and graffiti artists from across Britain have decorated it with an amazing mix of colours. Perhaps, not so colourful is 'shed' No.66170 en-route to Aberthaw with train 6O32 loaded coal hoppers from Onllwyn.

One artist may have publishing in mind, as CYMK (if I have interpreted the letters correctly) is the colour conversion RGB images conform to in this Book; **C**yan, **Y**ellow, **M**agenta and **K**ey (ie.Black).   **Chris Davies**

(above)

"A Day At The Races"

Having enjoyed a day at the races, Chester racecourse looks very pretty as FHH Class 66/5 No.66563 heads into a week-long engineer's possession (and past the winning post!) on the Wrexham line with 'JNA' ('Falcon') bogie ballast wagons from Crewe. A balanced composition with much to see in the foreground, as well as the train on the arches.

Chester Racecourse, known as the 'Roodee', is according to official records, the oldest racecourse still in use in England. Horse racing at Chester dates back to the early sixteenth century and is also thought to be the smallest racecourse of significance in England at 1 mile and 1 furlong long.   **Alan Hazelden**

"All Things Must Pass"

After passing the camera, an unidentified DBS Class 66/0 (above) pulls into the 'Run Round / Down Reception' line at Worksop with a loaded train of coal from Immingham, destined for either Cottam or West Burton power station. The main running lines look like quite a 'roller coaster'.

DBS 'tug' No.60001 (below) turns up the heat as it climbs through the cutting at New Mills Central with 6H43, the 07:46 Pendleton - Tunstead stone empties, excellently framed with a "closed in" feel. The colours appear slightly saturated but the flora is surprisingly lush here, presumably as a result of the warm stone and shelter from the elements. **David Hayes (2)**

"A Nice Pair"

Simple, but carefully composed, to give two contrasting compositions of a pair of Colas locos.

The yellow, orange & black colours look great on the Colas 37s and No.37219 + No.37175 (above) cross the River Severn at Eckington, running as 0Z37, Barry Docks - Kings Norton. Perhaps, considered to be a 'hackneyed' location, but still pleasing on the eye nonetheless. **Simon Howard**

Meanwhile, Colas Class 66/8s No.66847 and No.66850 (below) stand side by side in Eastleigh Yard waiting to work their next assignments. **Mark Pike**

"Close To The Edge"

Running 218 minutes late, Colas Class 70 No.70804 (above) working 4C30, Aberthaw - Gloucester Yard coal empties, passes along the Glamorgan Heritage coastline at Fontygary in the Vale of Glamorgan. Patience rewarded, having waited over three hours, it's a great relief when the train finally arrives. **Chris Davies**

Hired-in by GBRf, Class 47s No.47812 + No.47843 'Vulcan' (below) head along the banks of the River Humber at Hessle Whelps with a Hull Coal Terminal - Doncaster Down Decoy Yard 'cripples' working, comprising a single biomass 'Covhop' wagon. The picture has been taken with a camera on a pole to give added elevation and the north tower (510ft high) of the Humber Bridge stands tall on the right. **Ian Ball**

"Five Bridges"

Class 66/0 No.66207 (above) is completely enclosed within the open, riveted, rectangular, steel framework of Keadby Bridge, as it crosses the River Trent at Althorpe with 4D14, Scunthorpe - Tees Yard rail train. Keadby (or The King George V) Bridge opened in May 1916 and is a Scherzer rolling lift bridge, carrying both road and rail traffic across the River Trent.   **Alan Padley**

A mixture of red, white and blue lights illuminate the Royal Border Bridge in Berwick and a streak of light represents Class 91 No.**91111** (below) crossing the viaduct with 1S24, the 16:00 London King's Cross - Edinburgh service. Very nice!   **Steven Brykajlo**

Now repainted in DBS corporate red livery and de-named, Class 60 No.60074 (above) crosses the River Trent at Nether Lock, Newark, with 6E54, the 10:39 Kingsbury - Humber empty petroleum tanks. Smoke billows from the sugar factory as the train prepares to cross the ECML (out of shot).   **Alan Padley**

(Overleaf) : Here, an altogether different view of the same bridge, but with Class 66/0 No.66116 'shooting the rapids' at the weir, heading west with 6M57, the 07.15 Lindsey - Kingsbury loaded tanks.   **David Hayes**

The railway bridge over the River Dee, near Shotton, was built by the Manchester, Sheffield and Lincolnshire Railway, opening in 1889. This interesting composition shows the bridge to good effect, as Drax branded Class 60 No.60066 (above) approaches with 6M30, Margam - Dee Marsh steel, as viewed from Hawarden Bridge station looking towards Shotton High level station.

The central section was designed as a swing bridge to allow shipping to pass, but no longer opens and is welded shut, although the rotating mechanism (hydraulic cylinders, drive chain and sprocket) is still visible beneath the bridge. The bridge is part of the Borderlands Line from Wrexham to Bidston.   **Colin Partington**

"Panorama"

'Heritage' railways provide a wealth of photographic opportunities and, as such, attract photographers by the score, the Keighley & Worth Valley Railway being a good example. During a special 1940s weekend, 'split-box', Class 37/0 No.**37075** (above) in two-tone grey livery passes the Mill complex at Oakworth.

The loco was bought for preservation by The Class 37 Loco Association in August 1999, although being officially withdrawn from stock in November 1999. It made its maiden passenger run in preservation on the Great Central Railway on 23rd July 2000 working the 11:00hrs Ruddinton - East Leake. **Alan Padley**

(Previous Page): DBS Class 60 No.**60044** runs along the quayside towards David Davies Road stopboard with 6B39, the 14:32 Barry Docks ABP Shipment - Newport Alexandra Dock Junction, containerised chemicals service. The vessel moored is the chemical and oil products tanker MV 'Bomar Quest'. **Peter Slater**

Brunel's famous station at Bristol Temple Meads dominates an otherwise unbroken vista of modern architecture, as Colas 'tug' No.**60076** (above) passes along the 'Down Through' line, while in charge of 6V54, the 06:14 Chirk Kronospan - Exeter Riverside empty timber carriers. The derelict ground in the foreground is the site of the old Bristol Bath Road diesel depot (82A). **Mark Pike**

"I see no Jerry" - British hardened field defences of World War II were small fortified structures, constructed as part of British anti-invasion preparations. They were popularly known as 'pillboxes', due to their shape, strategically sited, such as this one built on the south bank of the River Dee near the railway bridge at Shotton.

The wide angle and inclusion of the pillbox provides added interest as Class 60 No.60092 (above) comes off Hawarden Bridge with 6V75, the 09:30 Dee Marsh - Margam steel. **Colin Partington**

An unidentified Freightliner Class 70 (below) wheels an assortment of brightly coloured containers, forming 4O70, the 09:58 Cardiff Wentloog - Southampton 'liner, past the small village of Westerleigh. The 13C Parish Church of St. James the Great is seen overlooking the South Gloucestershire countryside. In the distance, the skyline is broken by the towers of the first Severn Crossing, which carries the M48 Motorway - you may have to look hard to find it! **Edward Gleed**

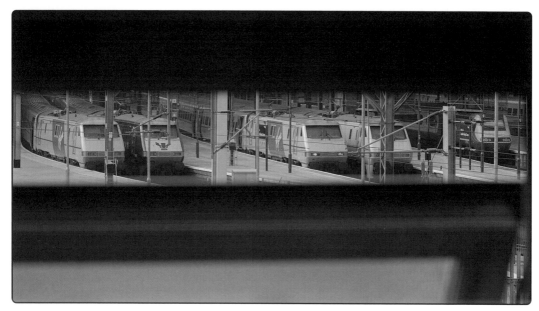

"Over Under Sideways Down"

An office window has been left sufficiently open to view a line up of trains waiting to leave London King's Cross station. These are headed by locos numbered **91113**, **91101**, **91114**, **91132** and **43064** (above), from left to right, respectively. An opportunity, well seized.   **Nigel Gibbs**

DBS Class 67 No.**67023** (below) is seen propelling 1W96, the 17:16 Cardiff Central - Holyhead away from Chester. Within three hours, between 18:00hrs - 21:00hrs, three Class 67 hauled passenger services can be seen at Chester; 1D31 to Llandudno, 1W96 to Holyhead and 1K96 to Crewe.   **Colin Partington**

DBS 'tug' No.60039 (above) crosses the River Trent at Newark, framed by the A46 Bypass and smoke trail from the British Sugar processing plant chimneys, with 6E46, the 04.37 Kingsbury - Lindsey discharged petroleum bogie tanks. The juxtaposition of all the angles really help the aesthetics of an image which has been well thought out.

Freightliner 'Fred', Class 66/5 No.66558 (above) nears journey's end as it crosses the Bridgewater Canal in Manchester with the late running 4H00, 07:27 Crewe Basford Hall - Trafford Park 'liner. The reflections of the buildings beside the canal shimmer on the water, as 'Jim' squats to take his picture.

The Bridgewater Canal connects Runcorn, Manchester and Leigh, commissioned by Francis Egerton, 3rd Duke of Bridgewater, to transport coal from his mines in Worsley to Manchester. It opened in 1761, initially from Worsley to Manchester, later extended from Manchester to Runcorn, then from Worsley to Leigh. The canal is connected to the Manchester Ship Canal via a lock at Cornbrook.   **David Hayes (2)**

"Synchronicity"

A close encounter of the third kind, so to speak .... DBS Class 60 No.60001 (above) working 6B47, Westerleigh - Robeston empty oil tanks and DRS Class 66/4 No.66429 working 4M36, Wentloog - Daventry 'Tesco Express', pass each other along the banks of the River Wye. Standing tall in the background is the First Severn Crossing suspension bridge, which carries the M48 Motorway.   **Chris Davies**

The number of freight services travelling between North Somerset Jct. and Dr. Day's Jct. are few and far between, seeing two pass each other is a rarity indeed. DBS Class 60 No.60019 'Port of Grimsby & Immingham' (below) is seen about to cross the feeder canal at North Somerset Jct. with the diverted 6B33, Theale - Margam discharged 'Murco' tanks, while Class 59 No.59102 'Village of Chantry' passes in the opposite direction atop 6A83, Avonmouth - Westbury loaded aggregate hoppers.   **Edward Gleed**

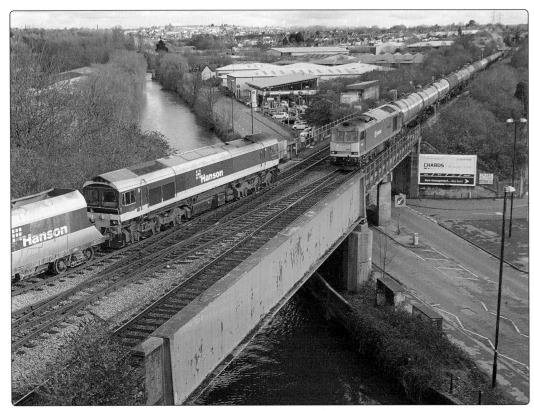

Viewed from Radwell, FHH Class 66/6 No.66601 (above) is seen on Sharnbrook viaduct waiting the road over Sharnbrook Jct. with 6Z45, 15:52 Luton - Mountsorrel, as East Midlands Train Class 222 'Meridian' DMU No.222009 passes on the 'Up Fast' with 1B61, the 16.05 Nottingham - London St Pancras.   **Nigel Gibbs**

Split second timing! This is Eastleigh at 14:10hrs on 4th August. No.450554 is waiting to depart with a Poole - London Waterloo 'stopping' service, No.444006 passes with a Weymouth - Waterloo 'semi-fast', No.444017 on a Waterloo-Weymouth 'semi-fast' and Class 70 No.70009 (below) undergoes a crew change with 4O49, the 09:22 Crewe Basford Hall - Southampton Maritime freightliner. Not a bad result!   **Mark Pike**

"Every Picture Tells A Story"

After being looped at Drem, GBRf Class 66/7 No.66736 'Wolverhampton Wanderers' (left) is seen ambling along the embankment, crossing over the A6137 with 6S45, the 06:25 North Blyth - Fort William loaded alumina tanks.

The inclusion of the road sign helps to place this shot - by the side of the B1377 road, near a roundabout at Ballencrieff.

Keith McGovern

"The Bends"

DBS Class 66/0 No.66186 (below), negotiates the reverse curves on the four track formation approaching Walsall station heading 6D44, the 11:09 Bescot Up Engineers Sidings - Toton North Yard departmental service. The composition accentuates the curves leading to Walsall South Junction in the foreground and, hidden behind the abundant vegetation, is a web of sidings backing onto Tasker Street, while the engineers have facilities on the right, hidden by the train, including a training facility. **John Whitehouse**

(opposite)
"Locked In" / "Rust Never Sleeps"

No.66119 (top right) scurries along the 'freight only' line next to the Sheffield & South Yorkshire Navigation Canal with 6M96, 13:21 Milford Sidings - Tunstead limestone 'empties' from Drax. The train is passing Kilnhurst Flood Lock and, despite its semi-dilapidated condition, the lock gates seem to be holding back the water, no doubt helped by the build up of detritus in front of the gates! **Alan Padley**

"Slippery When Wet"

Another 'shed', DBS Class 66/0 No.66133 (bottom right) struggles for adhesion on the wet rails as it climbs away from Walton Old Junction, approaching Warrington Bank Quay station with 6C38, Fiddlers Ferry - Newbiggin loaded gypsum. The colour light signal casts a long reflection on the saturated platform and note the adverse camber of the track where the loco comes onto the WCML. **Colin Partington**

"Another View"

A variation on a theme with cooling towers being brought into shot in differing ways. A 'wider' picture sees both the train and redundant cooling towers at Willington, the latter saved from demolition by colonised bats and other protected species. Colas 'grid' No.56087 (above) on 6S96, the 13:37 (ThO) Sinfin - Grangemouth discharged aviation fuel tanks is seen curving away from North Stafford Junction.   **John Whitehouse**

Further east, close to Willington level crossing, the cooling towers loom large above Class 60 No.60040 'The Territorial Army Centenary' (below), which is seen accelerating away from North Stafford Junction on the Uttoxeter line with 6Z37, 11:32 Ratcliffe PS - Warrington Arpley Sidings 'HTA' empties.   **Pauline McKenna**

(Opposite) : A long lens brings the cooling towers at Ferrybridge power station sharply into view, to provide an impressive backdrop for GBRf Class 66/7 No.66770, which is approaching Ulleskelf station on the 'Down Normanton' line with 4N93, Drax - Tyne Dock coal empties.

This image is a welcome departure from the 'classic' type of landscape orientation usually seen at this location and, whilst it's all a matter of choice, I personally prefer this portrait offering.   **Alan Hazelden**

Wherever possible, photographers tend to avoid locations where there are obtrusions, such as overhead wires and electricity pylons.

However, this need not be the case and results can be rewarding, if such situations are embraced and carefully thought out, as illustrated to good effect on this page.

Electrification is well advanced on the Liverpool - Earlstown line as Class 60 No.60011 (left) passes 77 Steps, Rainhill, with 6F26, Walton Old Junction - Liverpool BKTM empty 'HTA' coal hoppers.

A pylon looms large above the train supporting power lines which carry electricity that the next train of coal will help generate.

Colin Partington

"High Voltage"

The rape seed crop is looking about ready for harvest, as the blooms wave in the wind. Creating a contrast, is a pair of Freightliner Class 86s, powering north at Huddlesford, just south of Lichfield Trent Valley, heading 4M54, the 10:10 Tilbury - Crewe Basford Hall freightliner. A clash of liveries occur, with No.86622 in 'Powerhaul' livery leading No.86614 (above) in more traditional Freightliner green and yellow.

These fine workhorses started to be delivered to British Rail in 1965 and they are still going strong, plying their trade up and down the WCML, in what is the Class' 50th Anniversary year. **John Whitehouse**

"A Night's Tale"
(below)

Night shots always provide an interesting and challenging proposition, this view is no exception. It is well lit and the flower arrangement in the foreground gives added perspective.

After working a flask train to Valley, DRS Class 20s No.20308 + No.20305 (below) are seen running light engine alongside Platform 7 at Chester station, en route to Crewe Gresty Bridge for fuel. This pairing had previously worked 6K73, Sellafield - Crewe, followed by 6D41 to Valley.   **Colin Partington**

(Overleaf)
"Country Life"

Shades of yellow and orange! The Colas livery mirrors the oilseed rape at Uffington, as Class 60 No.60076 (page 218) runs along the Great Western Mainline with 6V62, the 10:44 Tilbury Riverside - Llanwern steel empties. The Met. Office had predicted a cloudy afternoon after a bright start but, fortunately, the cloud was later in arriving than forecast, resulting in some welcome sunshine. This carefully composed shot clearly demonstrates how a little thought and imagination can produce spectacular results.   **Martin Loader**

"A Momentary Lapse Of Reason"

The title is aimed at the author, rather than the photographer, for selecting an image (page 219) without a train anywhere to be seen, and why not? During the years spent producing 'Loco Review', I have seen thousands of splendid images on websites, but never one which has had over *50,000* views. This image is an exception and the reason why it's in the Book.

"Golden Hour" reflections at Wastwater in the Lake District .... what more needs to be said! **Syd Young**

"Framed"

Moving onto a 'heritage' railway - Keighley & Worth Valley Railway. The use of Mytholmes Tunnel has been used to frame Class 37/0 No.**37075** (above) as it prepares to pass through the 75 yards long tunnel, making its way to Keighley, during the KWVR's 1940s weekend in May. Mytholmes, between Oakworth and Haworth, is one of two tunnels on the line; the other is Ingrow Tunnel (150 yards long). **Alan Padley**

These Colas Tugs are getting everywhere ..... No.60087 'CLIC Sargent' (below) has just passed over Frodsham viaduct and prepares to rifle its way through Frodsham tunnel with 6J37, the 12:58 Carlisle - Chirk loaded log train. It's almost a case of not being able to see the wood for the trees....... **David Hayes**

A position of half way up the stairs on the footbridge at Acton Bridge station is taken to view oncoming freight trains from the north. In this case, the focus of attention is DBS Class 66/0 No.66092 (above) which is seen slowing to move onto the 'Up Slow' line with 6F62, the 11:12 Runcorn Folly Lane ICI Sidings - Warrington Arpley chemicals 'trip'.

This 'trip', along with the outward service (6F60), has to run to Northwich to reverse, as access to and from Folly Lane can only be made via Runcorn Junction, which is located just south of the 'Down' platform at Runcorn station. No.66092 will be seen again, heading north through Acton Bridge, about 60 minutes later.

Colin Partington

"Signals"

Snap 'em while you can .... semaphore signals are fast disappearing, as a result of a Network Operating Strategy, whereby all signalling in the UK will be Multiple Aspect colour lights (MAS), controlled from just 12 railway operating centres around the network. Sadly, the magnificent semaphores at Barnetby will be gone by the end of 2015.

A superb array of semaphores guard the approaches to Barnetby. DBS Class 66/0 No.66131 (above) passes Wrawby Junction with 6H77, the 16:30 Immingham - Drax loaded biomass, viewed from a foot crossing on the Brigg line, which affords a different view of the junction.   **Chris Davies**

Meanwhile, Class 66 No.66050 (below) passes Barnetby East signal box with 6T27, the 16:58 Immingham - Santon loaded iron ore tipplers.   **Martin Buck**

"Days Of Future Passed"

The UK's last independent coke works closes in December 2014 after failing to compete with cheaper Chinese rivals. Royston Coke Works, Yorkshire, had been making coke at Royston, near Barnsley, for over 130 years and received its coal supplies from the Hargreaves-owned Maltby Colliery (also now closed), a few miles away near Rotherham. It produced some 200,000 tonnes of coke per year, destined for use in glass, detergents and steel manufacturing. Unfortunately, flames (above) no longer burst into the sky, as unwanted gases are burnt off at Monckton coke works.   **Syd Young**

(overleaf) : In 2015, work commenced to demolish two well known industrial landmarks on the outskirts of Birmingham city centre; the gas holders at Washwood Heath. They were originally built in 1923 but, in the last 10 years, changes to the way gas is stored has made them surplus to requirements.

Here, a portrait format shot to remember the 213ft high gas holders, which once dominated the scene at Washwood Heath. FHH Class 66/5 No.66529, having run round its train, sets off with 4C03 to Crewe Virtual Quarry conveying concrete sleepers.   **David Hayes**